CENTER FOR JEWISH STUDIES
HARVARD JUDAIC TEXTS AND MONOGRAPHS
V

Harvard University
Center for Jewish Studies

Hasidism:
Continuity or Innovation?

Edited by
Bezalel Safran

Distributed by
Harvard University Press
*Cambridge, Massachusetts
and London, England*
1988

Library of Congress Cataloging-in-Publication Data
Main entry under title:

Hasidism : continuity or innovation?

(Harvard Judaic texts and studies; 5)
Bibliography: p.
Includes index.
1. Hasidism—History—18th century—Addresses, essays, lectures. 2.
Judah Loew ben Bezalel, ca. 1525-1609—Addresses, essays, lectures. I.
Safran, Bezalel, 1946-   . II. Series.
BM198.H273 1984   296.8'33   84-23892
ISBN 0-674-38120-3

Publication of this book was made possible by funds from the Wiliam
Landau Lecture and Publication Fund and from the Yanoff-Taylor
Lecture and Publication Fund, Harvard University Center for Jewish
Studies.

Printed by
Harvard University
Office of the University Publisher

TABLE OF CONTENTS

FOREWORD

The three studies contained in this volume are an outgrowth of a conference on early Hasidism entitled "Hasidism: Continuity or Innovation?" It was sponsored several years ago by Harvard University's Center for Jewish Studies, under the direction of Professor Isadore Twersky.

Many thanks to Carol Cross of Harvard University's Department of Near Eastern Languages and Civilizations for her patience and invaluable skill in preparing the photocopy of this volume for publication.

INTRODUCTION

Common to the articles presented here is a quest for perspectives on early Hasidic notions of spirituality.

E. Etkes deals with the Hasidic idea of *devekut*, communion with God, as it emerges out of its original historical context, focusing on its transformation from an abstract religious idea into a social force in the intimate circle of the Baal Shem Tov. Y. Hasdai provides a different context for Hasidic spiritual and social ideals: a common matrix—that of a "circle of Zadikim and Hasidim"—in which Beshtian Hasidism and Mitnagdism thrash out analogous religious and social ideologies. B. Safran suggests that eighteenth-century notions of Hasidic *devekut* become more meaningful and more sharply focused if viewed in light of the writings of the sixteenth-century Rabbi Judah Loew of Prague (Maharal).

There are wider ramifications to these different perspectives on early Hasidism.

Etkes begins with an assessment of previous studies on the social background which made it possible for the Hasidic message to generate a mass movement. Proceeding with his own inquiry, based on extant literary sources relative to the first generation, he questions the scholarly consensus that Hasidism was spawned as a popular movement. He finds rather that the Besht was cultivating a select group of already accomplished Hasidim who, with his emergence, turned to him as their guide and mentor. Still, the Besht himself may be said to have contributed to the transformation of Hasidism from an esoteric phenomenon into a popular movement through his extraordinary concern with Klal Yisrael. By committing himself to the welfare of the community (in ways that Etkes elaborates), the Besht provided a precedent which inspired his followers to abandon the pre-Beshtian Hasidic solitude in favor of an outer-directed impulse, a keen sense of accountability for the earthly needs of the people.

The upshot of the study is that it was not the needs of the masses which brought about the rise of Hasidism, nor did they determine its original nature. The genesis of the movement lies in exclusive circles, which gradually (by the third generation) open up to a wider community.[1]

In his treatment of the origins of the conflict between Hasidim and Mitnagdim. Y. Hasdai criticizes scholarly commonplaces accounting for Mitnagdism, the public opposition to the

Hasidic movement (which begins in Vilna, summer of 1772).

Studies of the conflict have tended to view "rebel" Hasidim confronting "Establishment" Mitnagdim from opposite poles of Jewish society. In the scenario which unfolds, Hasidim are deliberately raising either a social challenge, consciously providing an alternative to the leadership of the rabbis and *parnassim*; or a spiritual challenge, unsettling the traditional priorities, i.e., the supremacy of Torah study, and advocating instead the primacy of religious experience.

Hasdai's examination of a wide range of contemporary literary sources indicates the stereotypical "poles" simply do not exist. On the social plane, many of the rabbinic leaders are not party to anti-Hasidic opposition, and conversely, outstanding Hasidic leaders are not only not targeted in the polemical writing, but some of them are even treated with utmost respect in Mitnagdic books. Furthermore, social criticism in the Mitnagdic Derush literature is more trenchant than that of Hasidic writers, albeit out of concern and regret over the deterioration of the Jewish autonomy system. Conversely, Hasidic social criticism is limited only to the spheres in which the authority of the *Kehilla* has already been weakened. On the spiritual plane, too, there are Mitnagdim who are interested in disseminating Kabbalah among the general public, just as some Hasidim attempt to restrict Kabbalistic study to the movement's leaders.

Most striking is the emergence of the founders of Hasidism and active Mitnagdim from a common "circle of Zadikim and Hasidim" committed to overcoming the distance between scholars and the masses and energized by a sense of identification with the community's plight.[2] From within these common parameters, different approaches developed among Beshtian Hasidim and this circle. The debate over ideological differences might have continued with the communal leadership ultimately reconciling itself to the rise of Hasidism. But, Hasdai suggests, with the dissolution of the "Council of Four Lands" in 1764, the first partition of Poland in 1772, and the concomitant weakening of autonomous community leadership, the conditions were ripe for a public struggle between Mitnagdim and Hasidim: Hasidim could now be pointed to as aggravating the communal decline.

In his study on the influence of Maharal on early Hasidism, B. Safran examines the literary impact of an important late medieval writer on the vocabulary and thought structures of an early Hasidic writer. Rabbi Judah Loew of Prague (c. 1525-1609) wrote prolifically, but his writing mode is primarily exegetical, i.e., in clusters of interpretation on Rabbinic passages. His systematic views on given issues often have to be teased out by the reader.

Recent scholarship on the Maharal has explored a wide range of themes in his thought, even as it tries to determine its general direction. There have been works on his educational philosophy,[3] his eschatology,[4] his Kabbalistic background,[5] and his ethical and psychological assumptions;[6] studies on the Czech roots of his nationalist theories[7] as well as of his "anticipation" of modern philosophic notions;[8] accounts of his work as a halakist[9] as well as of the methodology of his Aggadah interpretation.[10] interpretation.[10]

Safran tries to locate Maharal's "center of vision" in his ethico-mystical thought, isolates and defines its central terms and motifs, and proposes an outline for understanding this thought as a coherent system. Maharal emerges as an exponent of a theory of *devekut*[11] where psychological insight, religious struggle and a mystical sense are crucial components. This account of *devekut* is centered on the notion of *ayin.*[12] Early Hasidism, in its attempt to present the Baal Shem Tov's spiritual way as a unified program, found Maharal's mystical vocabulary congenial and evocative. His usage of *ayin* and correlative terms are appropriated by Rabbi Menahem Mendel of Vitebsk (1730-1788), a representative early Hasidic writer of the school of the Magid of Mezeritch, as ethical-mystical categories.[13] Safran concludes that early Hasidim discovered that Maharal and they were fellow travelers in a common spiritual universe and made the most of his literary production.[14]

*   *

*

Both cumulatively and individually, these studies on the beginnings of the movement bear on an important historiographical concern which has preoccupied students of early Hasidism. Is the movement to be examined most usefully in context of the medieval period, or is it essentially a new departure in both social and intellectual history? Is Hasidism best understood in continuity with Jewish medieval spiritual movements or does it evidence "modernity" and a rupture of the old order? This question has generated much stimulating discussion.[15] The "perspectives" in this volume further advance the position that Hasidism should be viewed as an improvisation on familiar forms, an elaboration of historically identifiable ideas —even as it converts them into a powerful historical force.

Bezalel Safran

[1]The present study serves as an introduction—methodologically and thematically—to several other inquiries by Etkes. See his article, "Darko shel R. Shneur Zalman mi-Liadi ke-Manhig shel Hasidim," *Zion Jubilee Volume* L (1985), 321-354; and "Aliyato shel R. Shneur Zalman mi-Ladi l'Emdat Manhigut," *Tarbiz* LIV (1985), 429-439.

[2]A documented account of this circle—based on the *derushim* of R. Zevi Hirsch of Galena—is found in Y. Hasdai's article "'Eved ha-Shem be-Doram shel Avot ha-Hasidut," *Zion* XLVII (1982), 253-292. This study stimulates the suggestion that the circle served as a social and spiritual background for the development of Hasidism.

[3]A. F. Kleinberger, *ha-Mahashavah ha-Pedagogit shel ha-Maharal mi-Prag* (Jerusalem, 1962). Kleinberger elaborates the educational thought as a key to Maharal's *paideia*.

[4]B. Gross, Nezah Yisrael, *Hashkafato ha-Meshihit shel ha-Maharal mi-Prag 'al ha-Galut veha-Geulah* (Tel Aviv, 1974); R. Schatz, "Torat ha-Maharal bein Existenzia l'Eschatologia," in *Meshihiut v'Eschatologia* (Jerusalem, 1984), pp. 301-322.

[5]B. Sherwin, *Mystical Theology and Social Dissent: The Life and Works of Judah Loew of Prague* (Fairleigh Dickinson University Press, 1982).

[6]A Weiss, "Rabbi Loew of Prague: Theory of Human Nature and Morality" (Ph.D. dissertation, Yeshiva University, 1969). See his preface for previous treatments of this theme and chapter 11 for suggestions on "what is new in Rabbi Loew's theory of human nature and morality." Note the observation that the philosophical terms "matter" and "form" receive a psychological twist in Maharal's writings. This theme will be developed further in the present study. The most recent treatment of Maharal's moral thought is by M. Fox, "The Moral Philosophy of MaHaRaL," in *Jewish Thought in the Sixteenth Century*, ed. B. D. Cooperman (Harvard University Press, 1983), pp. 167-185.

[7]O. D. Kulka, "ha-Reka ha-Histori shel Mishnato ha-Leumit shel ha-Maharal mi-Prag," *Zion Jubilee Volume* L (1985), 277-320. The first effort to present Maharal in his own historical context, as a representative thinker of late medieval Jewish society, was made by Jacob Katz in a

stimulating analysis in a section of his *Masoret u-Mashber* (Jerusalem, 1958). Aspects of the analysis have generated discussion. See, for example, M. Breuer, "Vikuho shel ha-Maharal mi-Prag 'im ha-Noẓrim," *Tarbiz* LV (1986), 253-260.

[8]A. Neher, *Le Puits de l'Exil: La Théologie Dialectique du Maharal de Prague* (Paris, 1966). The work pinpoints a seminal theme in Maharal's thought, the theory of the *emẓ'a*, and develops it as the "humanism" of the Maharal.

[9]Y. Yudelov, "Teshuvot Maharal mi-Prag" in *Sefer ha-Zikkaron le-Maran R. Bezalel Zloty*, J. Buchsbaum, ed. (Jerusalem, 1987), pp. 264-296. See "Mavo" (pp. 264-269) for an assessment of Maharal as halakist.

[10]J. Elbaum, "Rabbi Judah Loew of Prague and his Attitude to the Aggadah," *Scripta Hierosolymitana* XXII (1971), 28-47.

[11]On *devekut* see G. Scholem, "Devekut, or Communion with God" in *The Messianic Idea in Judaism* (New York, 1971), pp. 203-227; B. Sherwin's review of the history of the term (citing previous bibliography) up to and including Maharal, op. cit., pp. 124-141; B. Safran, "Rabbi Azriel and Nahmanides: Two Views of the Fall of Man," in *Rabbi Moses Nahmanides (Ramban): Explorations in His Religious and Literary Virtuosity*, I. Twersky, ed. (Harvard University Press, 1983), pp. 75-106; M. Pachter, "The Concept of Devekut in the Homiletical Ethical Writings of Sixteenth Century Safed," in *Studies in Medieval Jewish History and Literature*, Vol. II, I. Twersky, ed. (Harvard University Press, 1984), pp. 171-230.

[12]Discussing the range of themes which bear on Maharal's notion of *devekut*—observance of mitzvot, study of Torah, faith, "full love of God"—B. Sherwin also refers (op. cit., p. 136) to Maharal's notion of "making oneself as if one is not" [*ayin*] in relation to God. This theme (central to R. Azriel of Gerona) he defines as negating

one's own being in relationship to God. A. Weiss (op. cit., pp. 343-344) similarly sees it as renouncing one's independent existence for the sake of God. The effect recognizes that in itself it is nothing; it exists only through the Cause. Weiss recognizes that this conception underlies some of the virtues discussed in *Netivot Olam* and goes on to interpret them accordingly.

The present study will amplify the account of *ayin* by a) indicating the significance of the term for Maharal's evocation of a state of *devekut*, b) clarifying the psychological basis of digressions "right" and "left" from the state of *devekut,* and c) relating select terms (*yosher, ayin, emẓ'a* and others) to this state.

[13]The mystical milieu suggested by the oft-repeated directives of the Magid of Mezeritch (and his school) —יבטל עצמו ממציאות; יחשוב עצמו לאין—was explored by R. Schatz in her study *ha-Hasidut ke-Mistika* (Jerusalem, 1980). Structuring the writings of the Magid and his disciples in categories borrowed from Christian quietism, she is able to show that self-annihilation is symptomatic of other quietist impulses in the thought of the Magid's school which were, however, controlled and restrained. Through this typological scheme, Schatz both organized the data and clarified some problems in the Magid's mysticism.

Another interpretive approach to the Magid is a "vertical" one. Can his mystical program be viewed as a link in the history of Jewish spirituality which preceded him? If so, might this have implications for the understanding of Hasidism as a whole? The study will suggest that the notion of *ayin* as a prerequisite to *devekut* is the orienting value of the Maharal's system and of that of a foremost disciple of the Magid, R. Menahem Mendel of Vitebsk.

For further discussion of *ayin* in early Hasidism, see J. Weiss, "Via Passiva in Early Hasidism," *Journal of Jewish Studies*, XI, Nos. 3,4 (1960).

[14]A sequel to this study will deal with the profound impact of Maimonides on early Hasidism as reflected in the book *Meor Eynim* by Rabbi Menahem Nahum of Chernobyl.

[15]For a critical survey of the range of approaches and bibliography, see Y. Hasdai's article, op. cit., pp. 253-258. For other recent studies exploring roots of Hasidism in the prevailing pietistic and intellectual milieu, see I. Tishbi, "'Ikvot R. Moshe Haim Luzzatto be-Mishnat ha-Hasidut," *Zion* XLIII (1978), 201-234, and M. Piekarz, *Bi-Mei Zemihat ha-Hasidut* (Jerusalem, 1978).

Hasidism as a Movement-The First Stage*
Emanuel Etkes

Historical research on the rise of the Hasidic movement has been characterized by the search for an adequate explanation of the emergence and striking expansion of the movement. It appears that a certain pattern of thought has developed among historians who dealt with these matters. The growth of Hasidism within a relatively short time into a popular movement encouraged those scholars to conclude that, from its very beginning, Hasidism rose as a response to a very deep need of the Jewish masses in Poland. Based upon this conclusion, the scholars made efforts to discover and describe the suffering of Polish Jewry during the first half of the eighteenth century and then proceeded to interpret Hasidism as a panacea for this situation. This pattern of thinking is best reflected in the works of Simon Dubnow and Benzion Dinur, the two historians who have proposed the most comprehensive interpretation for the beginning of Hasidism and whose views on these matters have had a wide impact.

1

Dubnow[1] found that the religious establishment of Polish Jewry, or what he called the rabbinical religion, experienced a severe crisis during the period prior to the emergence of Hasidism. According to Dubnow, the task of religion was to provide spiritual support to the suffering individual. During this period, the Jew's suffering became more overwhelming, for it was then that the Christian burghers intensified their struggle against Jewish merchants and artisans; the Polish shlachta extended their exploitation and suppression of the Jews living within its territories, while the Catholic Church broadened its propaganda and encouraged new blood libels. It was not only that the so-called "rabbinical religion" did not fulfill its mission by helping the suffering Jews during these years, but that this religion itself now became an oppressive factor. In Dubnow's words,

> The rabbinate gave the people religious government rather than religious faith. It organized Jewish life into a vast number of customs, detailed religious practices, and prohibitions, the observance of which was difficult....Most of those severe rabbinical injunctions were unconnected with faith, and the simple Jew found no satisfaction for his simpler religious feelings.[2]

Hasidism filled the vacuum left by 'rabbinical religion' by providing a religious framework which met the intellectual level and emotional needs of the common Jew. However, this popularization of Judaism was accompanied by a certain vulgarization. Again, in Dubnow's words,

> While it is true that for that purpose Hasidism made use of some imaginary visions and superstitions, tales of wonders and miracles, the cult of "Tzadikim," exemplary figures who mediated between man and God...nevertheless, in that it brought Judaism down from the world of "Atsilut" to lower regions and placed it within the reach of the average man, even of the common man, Hasidism succeeded in attracting great masses of followers.[3]

The plight of Polish Jewry received a different portrayal in the work of Benzion Dinur.[4] According to Dinur, it was the communal organization which suffered a deep functional crisis during the first half of the eighteenth century. A small group of wealthy Jews usurped the leadership of the communal organiation. These corrupted leaders exploited the kehillah organization in order to extend their power and wealth. As a result of this economic and social oppression, the gap between the masses and the ruling class became more manifest. This was the background for the appearance of a social opposition which attempted to challenge the communal establishment. This opposition failed, yet it was Hasidism which emerged as an extension of this opposition, which gave expression to the social protest of the masses.

Furthermore, Dinur claimed that Hasidism responded also to messianic expectation, left unfulfilled following the Sabbatean failure. The Besht discovered that it was possible to hasten the redemption by elevating Klal Yisrael to the level of 'dor deah.' While the sixteenth-century kabbalists of Safed attempted to bring the Messiah through the spiritual achievements of a very limited elite, the Besht thought that this goal would not be achieved unless the masses reached the proper spiritual level. The Besht's efforts to teach Hasidism among the people were therefore motivated by a Messianic desire and a Messianic plan.

Although Dubnow and Dinur differ with regard to the nature of the suffering of the Jewish masses in Poland and with regard to the solutions offered by Hasidism, they both agreed that Hasidism was basically a popular movement in the sense that its emergence and expansion were directly related to the suffering of the masses. Upon this common premise, it is only natural to find that both Dubnow and Dinur described the Besht as a leader who was active in preaching Hasidism to the masses.[5]

As is well known, the views of Dubnow and Dinur have been widely discussed and criticized by later scholarship. Some elements of their interpretation have been questioned, while others were rejected. A large-scale examination

of their views on Hasidism are of course beyond
the limits of this paper; however, I would like to
focus on one basic element. What I have in
mind is the common view of Dubnow and
Dinur regarding the popular nature of the
Hasidic movement from its inception. Allow
me to raise several questions.

Is it valid to assume that the emergence of the
Hasidic movement was closely connected to the
suffering of the Jewish masses in Poland? Was
Hasidism shaped from the outset in order to
meet the needs of the masses? Did the Besht
carry a religious message for the average Jew?

We shall be able to appreciate the full
significance of these questions after we pay
attention to the phenomenon of pre-Beshtianic
Hasidism and the connection between it and the
Besht.

Individuals and small groups of Hasidim
prior to the Besht were inspired and directed by
the heritage of the sixteenth-century kabbalists
of Safed. Dinur already has shown that such
groups existed close to the Besht. Moreover, he
found that some of the Besht's disciples had
previously belonged to the old type of
Hasidism.[6]

The nature of the pre-Beshtianic Hasidim
and their relationship with the Besht has been
discussed in further detail by Scholem and
Weiss. Scholem found that close to the
revelation of the Besht a new type of Hasidim
appeared. These Hasidim differed from the

previous Hasidim by the ecstatic nature of their
prayer, by their reserved attitude toward
aesceticism and Halachic study.[7] Needless to
say, these characteristics remind us of
Beshtianic Hasidism. Josef Weiss, in his
reconstruction of the Hasidic group in Kotev,
pointed out some similarities between this
group and Beshtianic Hasidism.[8] M. Piekarz, in
his book *Bimei Tsmiḥat HaHasidut*, also
discovered the similarity between Hasidic
teachings and the writings of authors who,
while not part of the Hasidic movements, can be
characterized as Hasidim of the old type.[9]

From the research on the pre-Beshtianic
groups of Hasidim and the similarities and
connections between these groups and the
Besht, it becomes apparent that the Besht and
his group did not emerge from a vacuum. On
the contrary, within the framework of their time
and place, the Besht and his disciples emerge as
only a part of a much wider phenomenon of
Hasidism. In the light of these conclusions, we
can appreciate the revolutionary nature of
Beshtianic Hasidism. While Hasidism prior to
the Besht was a phenomenon of outstanding
individuals, or of very limited and exclusive
groups, Beshtianic Hasidism became a wide,
popular movement.

The question which the historian of Hasidism
should therefore deal with is, how and why
indeed did these transformations take place.
We can divide this question into two: 1) what

motivated the Hasidic elite to abandon its way
and to commit itself to the leadership of the
masses? 2) why were the masses attracted to this
new leadership? Why did they acknowledge its
authority and adopt its way of worshiping God?

In this paper I will only relate to the first of
these questions and only to the more specific
contexts of the Besht's period. Therefore the
question which will direct my discussion is this:
had the transformatin of Hasidism from an
esoteric phenomenon into a popular movement
already begun during the Besht's lifetime, and,
if so, what was the Besht's contribution to this
process?

Following an examination of the sources
describing the Besht's public activity, mostly
the stories in *Shivhei HaBesht* and the
"drushim" (homiletic sermons) which were
brought by Yacov Yosef, it seems to me that we
can distinguish among three main circles of
activity which characterized the Besht's life: 1)
the Besht as Baal Shem, 2) the Besht as a carrier
of a religious message, and 3) the Besht's care
for Klal Yisrael.

The activity of the Besht as a Baal Shem was
clarified and described by Scholem.[10] By
proving that the Besht was active until the end
of his life as a Baal Shem, Scholem rejected the
attempts, both by Hasidism and by scholars, to
blur these facts.

As a Baal Shem, the Besht used the same
means common among other Baalei Shem

during those generations: amulets, magic spells, and charms. And yet the Besht possessed some very unique spiritual powers which were not possessed to the same extent by other Baalei Shem. What I have in mind are powers such as telepathy, clairvoyance, the capability to communicate with ghosts, and so forth. It is important to point out that, while the Besht did use these powers for his activities as a Baal Shem, he also used them for other purposes. Therefore, the use of supernatural powers is not a sufficient criteria to define the limits of the Besht's activities as a Baal Shem. We need additional criteria. The Besht acts as a Baal Shem when he provides a personal service upon the request of others, and usually for payment.

Did the Besht's activities as a Baal Shem play a decisive role regarding the foundation of Hasidism? Needless to say, if the Besht had been *only* a Baal Shem, he would not have become the founder of Hasidism. We know about other famous Baalei Shem who did not leave behind them a spiritual movement. Yet one can suggest that the Besht gained at least part of his reputation and authority as a result of his fame as a Baal Shem. This possibility is apparently proved by some of the stories in *Shivhei HaBesht.*[11] In one of these stories we are told that the Mochiah of Polna became an admirer of the Besht after he witnessed the Besht's magical skills.[12] Scholem suggests that this is an authentic story.[13] However, we know about other close friends and disciples of the Besht who reacted negatively towards his activities as a Baal Shem. For example, Zeev Kutses and David Furkes became disciples of the Besht, not because of his magical capabilities, but despite them.[14]

It is possible to sum up that the magical skills of the Besht did not play a direct role and certainly not a decisive one regarding the rise of Hasidism. Yet, it seems quite possible that these skills, when they joined with the other characteristics of the Besht, attracted at least some of his disciples and admirers.

Let us now turn to examine the second circle in which the Besht was active. There is no doubt that the Besht was active as a carrier of a religious message and served as a guide in the worship of God. He functioned as such, not only because the people around him and close to him saw him as an ideal model which should be followed, but also because he himself felt a deep desire to share his mystical experiences with others. But this activity of the Besht never went beyond the very restricted limits of a small group, a group which should be called the Besht's circle.

The most interesting attempt to characterize the Besht's circle was done by Josef Weiss. According to Weiss, the atmosphere of the circle was shaped by an acute spiritual crisis. The members of the circle believed that they had failed in their efforts to elevate the people.

In their discussions they focused on the reasons for this failure and on finding new means of influence. Weiss claimed that these discussions became the core of the concept of the Tsadik.

It seems to me that the attractive picture drawn by Weiss leaves much room for critical examination, to some extent already done by Piekarz.[15] For the purpose of our discussion, I will limit myself here to one methodological remark. Weiss focused on the themes and the ideological tendencies common to the members of the circle, but he did not pay enough attention to the issue of the personal contacts between the members of the circle and the Besht. His portrayal of the circle serves the demands of the historian of ideas; however, it cannot satisfy the historian who is interested in the Besht's circle as the nucleus from which the Hasidic movement emerged.

It seems to me that the sources provide a solid basis to conclude that there were indeed groups of people who can be rightly called the Besht's circle. Moreover, these groups can be characterized by three main features:

1. Personal and intimate contact between each member of the group and the Besht.

2. A common spiritual and religious orientation shared by the group and the Besht.

3. Recognition of the spiritual superiority of the Besht by all members of the group.

Let us now examine these criteria in detail.

The personal contact between the individuals in the circle and the Besht was neither permanent nor continuous. As is well known, the Besht was inclined to constant travel, while his followers were never concentrated in one location. It is therefore obvious that most of the circle could not remain in constant contact with their leader. Yet, we read in *Shivhei HaBesht* about various patterns of contact between the Besht and individuals in his circle. Those who lived in Medzibezh, for example, used to meet him in the Beit HaMidrash and would visit him at home.[16] Those who lived far away used to visit the Besht occasionally and would spend with him a Shabbat, a holiday, or even a few weeks. The Besht himself tended to visit his disciples while travelling around the country.[17] From other stories in *Shivhei HaBesht*, we learn that the members of the group had "se'uda shlishit" together in the Besht's house.[18] It seems that these types of meetings were still of an occasional nature and had yet to crystallize into a permanent institution. All and all, it would seem that, although individuals of the circle were not constantly close to the Besht, the experience of personal and intimate contact with him played a critical role in shaping their relationship.[19]

When we examine the nature and the background of the people who had close contact with the Besht and who saw him as their guide, we found that many of them had already been Hasidim before meeting the Besht. Gershon Kotover, the Besht's brother-in-law, was connected to the famous klaus of Brody.[20] Nachman of Kosov, and the mochiah of Polna, belonged to the circle of Hasidim in Kotov.[21] Nachman of Horodenko admits that he was a great Hasid even before he knew the Besht.[22] We have reason to believe that this was also the case regarding Ze'ev Kutses, David Furkes, the Magid of Mezrich and others.[23] It seems to me quite reasonable that, from what we know about the background of those disciples of the Besht, we can extrapolate about the rest. If this evaluation is correct, then one can maintain that it was not the Besht who turned the members of the group into Hasidim, but rather the contrary—as they were already Hasidim, they were motivated to acknowledge the Besht's leadership. In other words, their recognition of the Besht's authority was based on a common spiritual background and religious ideas, shared by them and the Besht. It was within the framework of this spiritual partnership that the unique virtues of the Besht became so prominent.

Acknowledgement of the unique virtues of the Besht is, as I suggested before, the third criterion for belonging to the Besht's circle.

It seems that different aspects of the Besht's personality attracted different people. Rabbi Nachman of Horodenko became a disciple of the Besht after he learned from him how to overcome "machshavot zarot."[24] Previously, Rabbi Nachman failed in his efforts to cope with this obstacle through aesceticism, the means which were common in pre-Beshtianic Hasidism. The Magid was attracted to the Besht after he saw how the Besht had turned the study of Kabbalah into a mystical experience.[25] This happened right after the Magid himself had failed to study Kabbalah on the same *madraigah*, spiritual level. HaMochiach of Polna claimed that he possessed some unique spiritual powers, but he acknowledged the superiority of the Besht in this matter and tried to learn from him.[26] Needless to say, the individuals around the Besht were attracted by his ecstatic prayers, by his ability to communicate with ghosts, by his *aliyot neshamot* and so forth, but these unique spiritual aspirations were shared by the group members themselves. It seems to me true, to sum up, that the group acknowledgment of the Besht's superior abilities was derived from the fact that he succeeded in concretizing in a most exceptional way the same ideas which attracted the group members. The significance of the Besht's message for his disciples was not, therefore, the claim to accept Hasidism as an ideal but rather the presentation of an exemplary model of these ideals.

It will be, I believe, quite fruitful to point out an important exception which proved the rule. What I have in mind is the case of Yaacov Yosef

of Polna. The tradition relating to Yaacov
Yosef's transformation into a disciple of the
Besht tells us explicitly that, prior to his meeting
with the Besht, Yaacov Yosef was *not* a Hasid
and that he adopted the Hasidic manner only
after this encounter.[27] Before he became a
Hasid, Yaacov Yosef was a communal rabbi
and a scholar of the traditional type. While
staying with the Besht, Yaacov Yosef
experienced for the first time in his life a very
moving and heartbreaking prayer. This was
followed by a change in Yaacov Yosef's scale of
values. Ecstatic prayer as a means to achieve
intimate contact with God now became his
supreme value, while traditional scholarship
lost its previous superiority.

This spiritual revolution is appropriately
expressed in the saying related to Yaacov Yosef
himself:

> I heard from the Rabbi who used to say:
> "The tsaddik Yaacov Yosef, God bless his
> memory, used to say that it was easier for
> him to discuss ten subtle halakic questions
> than to say the eighteen benedictions one
> time."[28]

The testimony about how Yaacov Yosef
became a Hasid teaches us two lessons. First,
the fact that *Shivhei HaBesht* found it necessary
to insist that Yaacov Yosef was not a Hasid
until his first meeting with the Besht enforces
our impression that most of the Besht's
disciples were already Hasidim before he met

them. Secondly, when the Besht was active in turning a non-Hasid into a Hasid, the person in question belongs to the intellectual elite.

Was the Besht also active in teaching Hasidism among the masses? As may be recalled, this was the view held by Dubnow and Dinur. Scholem refrained from going so far. However, in his classic article on 'Devekut,' he suggested that the Besht expected every Jew to reach 'Devekut' or at least try to.[29]

It seems to me that the views of Dubnow, Dinur and Scholem require serious amendment. My criticism is supported by the following considerations:

1. In the many stories about the Besht's travels and his contacts with the public, there is no mention whatsoever about his attempts to teach Hasidic methods of worship to the masses.

2. The idea that every Jew should endeavor to achieve Devekut is so revolutinary in contrast to the traditional Kabbalistic conception of Devekut that we can expect an explicit expression of this idea by the Besht. But the quotation which Scholem brought to support his view may be interpreted in several ways, and none of them include such a clear expression.[30]

3. When we examine the drushim of the Besht—mostly those brought by Yaacov Yosef—we realize that these drushim reflect the Besht's personal experience as a mystic. His longing to achieve an intimate and permanent contact with God, his wondering regarding the

obstacles which prevent him from realizing his desire, the means which he developed in order to overcome these obstacles, and the unique experience of achieving close and intimate touch with the upper worlds.

It would be quite unreasonable to assume that the Besht directed these drushim to the masses. On the contrary, it seems much more logical that they express the Besht's needs to share his experience and achievements with the small group of his disciples or with other groups of Hasidim—those who were his spiritual partners, if not in achievement, at least in desires.

This evaluation is supported by the same document upon which Dubnow and Dinur base their views. In his letter to his brother-in-law, R. Gershon,[31] the Besht described *'aliyat Neshama,'* during which he met the Messiah. In reply to the Besht's question, "When are you coming?" the Messiah replied, "When what you have learned is revealed in the world and your inner sources flow out and spread what I have taught you and they too can make 'Yiḥudim' like you."

Dubnow and Dinur interpreted these words as reflecting the Besht's desire to spread the message of Hasidism,[32] but they overlooked the Besht's response,

> And I felt great sadness at the length of time until that could come to be. But from what I learned when I was there, three

"segulot," three holy names, and they are
easy to learn and interpret, my mind
became cooler and I thought that by that
means people like me could also ascend to
that high level and be like me.
The teaching which the Besht accepted from the
Messiah is probably a special technique for
Yihudim. The possibility that such a mystical
experience could be practiced by the masses
seemed to the Besht impractical. Yet, he hoped
that *bnei gilo* or the members of his circle would
be able to reach this *madraigah* with the
assistance of certain holy names he would
reveal to them.

To sum up, the Besht did not go beyond the
traditionally accepted conception of his age and
of previous ages; namely, that worshiping God
on the level of Hasidism was appropriate for
only outstanding individuals and was not
within the reach of the masses. His role as a
carrier of a religious message was therefore
restricted only to the very limited group of his
friends and disciples. Yet there is no doubt that
the ecstatic prayer of the Besht made a deep
impression upon simple Jews as well, with its
outer manifestations.

Thus far we have discussed the Besht's
activities as a Baal Shem and as a guide in the
worship of God. Let us now turn to the third
area in which he was active: care and support
for Klal Yisrael. There were two foundations at
the basis of this activity:

1. A consciousness of mission regarding the fate of Klal Yisrael.
2. Unique spiritual powers which he possessed and through which he could foresee future troubles and interfere with the course of events.

The starting point for the Besht's activities for Klal Yisrael was in most cases some sort of revelation. At times it was a revelation about an impending danger and at times about a dangerous event occurring at the same time in a distant place. The techniques of revelations are various. He hears *karozim*, he communicates with ghosts, uses his power of clairvoyance, practices aliyat neshamah, and so forth.

The missions the Besht takes upon himself are also various—some in the methaphysical sphere and some in the earthly sphere. For example, the Besht traveled into the upper worlds in order to cancel a decree that the Torah will be taken away from the people of Israel. On his way the Besht discovered many prayers which had not reached their destination. They asked for his help.[33] Another example of activity in the metaphysical sphere is the correction of the souls of sinners who passed away before repentance.[34] In the earthly sphere the Besht attempted to prevent blood libels or at least to soften their results, to save a Jewish community from an attack by by-passing military forces, to expel thieves who once dwelled in a certain forest, and so forth.[35] Two other important matters with which the Besht dealt in the earthly sphere—ritual slaughter and the redemption of prisoners—were discussed and clarified in Professor Shmeruk's illuminating articles.[36]

It is important to point out once again that most of the Besht's efforts in these various matters were connected with his unique spiritual powers. This is the case even when he dealt with a halachic problem like *shchitah*, ritual slaughter. The Besht heard a *karoz*, heavenly signal, that he should fire a certain *shochet*, ritual slaughterer. He discovered that the *shochet* was overly strict in pronouncing an animal as unkosher and found him unconcerned with the financial damage which was caused by his decision. In order to stress his opinion that the animal was kosher, the Besht asked to eat from the animal although he did not justify this strange request with any halachic considerations. Instead, he justified his request by his special power to see that the animal was kosher or, in his words, "that animal is asking me to eat it."[37]

As I have said before, the Besht's concern for Klal Yisrael was motivated by a sense of mission. This sense was nourished both by the Besht's feeling of solidarity with the fate of his people and his acknowledgment that the unique spiritual powers he was endowed with were granted to him in order to serve Klal Yisrael. This element of the Besht's self-image is well reflected in the Besht's explanation that his failure to foresee the blood libels in Zosliv stemmed from a heavenly punishment.[38] In his inclination to interfere with the course of events, the Besht looms as an activist who rejects the passivity apparently demanded by the value of *bitachon*, trust in God. This characteristic of the Besht is well pronounce in the following story:

> It was the custom of Rabbi Naḥman of Horodenka to say about everything that he saw or everything that befell him that it is for the best. His faith was as strong as an iron pillar.
>
> Once they drafted soldiers from among the Jews of the holy community of Medzhibozh. The Besht said to him: "Pray that they do not draft soldiers from the Jews."
>
> He said to him that it was for the best. The Besht said to him: "It is good that you did not live in Haman's time because you would have said that his decree was good as well. The only good that came of it was that they hanged Haman—which was for the best."[39]

Finally, it is important to point out a further characteristic of the Besht's activities for Klal Yisrael: his unique sensitivity toward the weak elements in society. This sensitivity showed itself in his willingness to forgive sinners whose behavior was motivated by economic or mental suffering. In *Shivhei HaBesht*, we are told of cases when the Besht preferred to ignore the sins of such people or had made efforts to encourage them to repent.[40]

Let us now sum up the main conclusions which can be drawn from this paper.

We have claimed that the Besht attempted to spread neither Hasidic teachings nor Hasidic customs among the wide public. On the contrary, the size and nature of the Besht's circle manifests a continuity with the traditional view—that is, the worshiping of God in the *madraigah* of Hasidism is only appropriate for outstanding individuals. Thus, the description presented by both Dubnow and Dinur, according to which Hasidism was a popular movement already from its inception, is unacceptable.

In spite of this conclusion, we still had to face the question whether, and in what sense, the Besht himself contributed to the transformation of Hasidism from an esoteric phenomenon into a wide and popular movement. Here we offered a positive answer by stressing the Besht's concern for Klal Yisrael. By committing himself to the fate and welfare of Klal Yisrael, the Besht provided a precedent which inspired his disciples and followers. The inclination of the pre-Beshtian Hasidim towards solitude and separation, an inclination immanent to the tradition of Kabbalistic elites, was now replaced by a conception of care and responsibility for the earthly needs of the public. That and more, the Besht also provided a pattern of leadership which became a model to be followed by his disciples. The phenomenon of a charismatic personality who utilized his special powers in order to serve the daily needs of his public, the phenomenon which later became a prominent feature in Hasidic leadership, has its origins in the Besht's personality and activity.

Finally, I would like to relate in a few words to the following stages in the development of Hasidism as a popular movement. During the sixties, under the guidance of the Magid, Hasidism successfully spread its teachings to the public; yet, it seems to me that even during this stage there was no attempt to reach the masses. Hasidism, it would seem, focused its efforts even then on the more educated elements of society.

The popular element became a significant part of the Hasidic movement only in the third generation of its existence, the generation of the Magid's disciples. The two circles of activity which had lived separately during the Besht's period were now united into one whole: that community, for whom the Hasidic leader strives to solve its earthly problems, is that same community in which the Hasidic leader serves as a model and guide in the worship of God. This development is clearly expressed in the writings of Yaacov Yosef, published in the 1780s, although probably reflecting the seventies; Yaacov Yosef questions whether it is possible to bridge the gap between the high standards of Hasidic worship of God and the poor spiritual level of the masses. Hasidism's response was the institution and the theory of the Tzadik. It is by no means an accident that the theory of the Tzadik became a central theme only in the writings of the Magid's disciples.

In conclusion, I would like to suggest that it was not the needs of the masses which brought about the emergence of Hasidism nor did they shape its original nature. The history of Hasidism is rather a story of a movement whose values and patterns were derived initially from a tradition of exclusive and esoteric circles. Therefore, in order to become eventually a popular movement, Hasidism had to undergo a gradual process of adjustment. It seems to me that the full story of this complicated and fascinating process has yet to be told.

*I wish to thank the Memorial Foundation for Jewish Culture for granting me a fellowship to help in the research and writing of this paper.

[1]Professor Dubnow presented his views concerning the factors that brought about the growth and expansion of Hasidism extensively in the introduction to his *History of Hasidism* (Hebrew). In the following notes I refer to the edition published in Tel Aviv in 1960.

[2]Dubnow, p. 23.

[3]Dubnow, p. 3.

[4]See Benzion Dinur, "The Origins of Hasidism and its Social and Messianic Foundations," in *The Course of Generations* (Jerusalem, 1956; Hebrew), pp. 83-227.

[5]See Dubnow, pp. 48, 51-52, 59-60; Dinur, pp. 181-188.

[6]See Dinur, pp. 159-170.

[7]See Gershom Scholem, "The Two Earliest Documents of the Circles of Hasidim and the Besht," *Tarbiz* 20 (1950).

[8]See J. G. Weiss, "A Circle of Pneumatics in Pre-Hasidism," *Journal of Jewish Studies*, VIII (1957).

[9]Jerusalem, 1978.

[10]See Gershom Scholem, "The Historical Image of the Besht," *Molad* (Av-Elul, 1960; Hebrew), 144-155. Also in *Devarim Bego* (collected essays, Hebrew; Jerusalem, 1975), pp. 287-324.

[11]Quotations from *Shivhei HaBesht* are taken from the edition of Benyamin Mintz (Jerusalem, 1969).

[12]*Shivhei*, p. 124.

[13]See Scholem, "Historical Image," in *Devarim Bego*, p. 296.

[14]On their reservations regarding the Besht because he was a Baal Shem, see *Shivhei*, p. 121. Their positive attitude towards the Besht appears in a number of stories; see, for example, pp. 110, 128, 129, 134 in *Shivhei*.

[15]See Mendel Piekarz, *When Hasidism was Flourishing* (Hebrew; Jerusalem, 1978), especially chapter 3.

[16]See *Shivhei*, pp. 61, 62, 63, 134.

[17]See *Shivhei*, pp. 66, 96-97, 118, and elsewhere.

[18]*Shivhei*, pp. 75, 143, 144, 153, 155.

[19]That is most evident in the stories describing how the Besht's circle drew near him. See *Shivhei*, pp. 58-59, 66, 75-76, and others. It would seem that the intimate personal bond between the Besht and some of his circle is expressed in the appellation "anshei segulato." See *Shivhei*, pp. 75, 1154, and others.

[20]I learned of that from the valuable work of Elhanan Reiner on the Kloiz of Brod, which has not yet been published.

[21]See J. Weiss, "Circle."

[22]See *Shivhei*, p. 112.

[23]R. Zeev Kutses and R. David Furkes are described in *Shivhei* as men who had been Hasidim before they knew the Besht. See *Shivhei*, p. 121. The Magid of Mezrich had been accustomed to mortify himself and was involved with Kabbala before meeting the Besht. See *Shivhei*, pp. 75-76.

[24]See note 22, above.

[25]The two versions of the way the Magid approached the Besht are quite different from each other in many details, but they have a common core. See *Shivhei*, pp. 75-76; also see the end of the second part of *Keter Shem Tov* (Bnei Brak, 1956), p. 81.

[26]*Shivhei*, pp. 66, 125, 154-155.

[27]*Shivhei*, p. 66.

[28]*Shivhei*, p. 101.

[29]See G. Scholem, "Devekut, or Communion with God," in *The Messianic Idea in Judaism* (New York, 1971), pp. 208-209.

[30]Scholem, "Devekut," bases his argument on the fact that the Besht identifies Devekut with Emuna (faith), an idea which implies that the descent from a situation of Devekut is like the denial of the existence of God. It would seem that that idea expresses the Besht's yearnings for constant Devekut, but there is no reason to conclude that the Besht considered that high spiritual level to be accessible to every Jew.

[31]"Igeret HaKodesh," which was written by the Besht to R. Gershom of Kotov, was first printed by R. Yaacov Yosef of Polno at th end of his book, *Ben Porat Yosef* (Koritz, 5541 [1781]).

[32]See Dubnow, p. 60; Dinur, pp. 181-183.

[33]*Shivhei*, pp. 63-64, 62, 157.

[34]*Shivhei*, pp. 65-66; "Igeret HaKodesh" (n.31 above) was appended to Mintz's edition of *Shivhei*, p. 167.

[35]See *Shivhei*, pp. 115, 127, 153, 128, 137-138, 126, 143 "Igeret HaKodesh," pp. 168-169.

[36]See Chone Shmeruk, "The Social Significance of Hassidic Ritual Slaughtering" (Hebrew), *Zion* 20, 47-72; also Shmeruk, "Hasidism and the Leasing of Property" (Hebrew), *Zion* 35, 182-192.

[37]*Shivhei*, p. 117.

[38]*Shivhei*, p. 74.

[39]*Shivhei*, pp. 117-118.

[40]*Shivhei*, pp. 79, 116, 125.

THE ORIGINS OF THE CONFLICT BETWEEN HASIDIM AND MITNAGDIM
Yaacov Hasdai

In the summer of 1772, the Jewish community of Vilna sent a letter to the main Jewish communities in Poland. The letter speaks of a group of despicable hypocrites called *Hasidim*. These people are said to spurn Torah study and to hold Torah scholars in contempt. They are said to spend their time in all kinds of frivolity; they gesticulate strangely when they pray; they meet for prayer separately from the established congregations.

The letter relates that the actions of these people have caused the Vilna community considerable trouble. Therefore, the letter continued, the heads of the community met and decided to uproot this new wickedness. They punished the group's leaders, including a man who had been a local *magid*, they burned the group's books at the gate of the synagogue, and issued a ban forbidding the group to hold separate prayer services.

The letter urges all the other Jewish communities to act likewise and to destroy the *Hasidic* groups that may have sprung up in their midst.

This letter launched the struggle against the new *Hasidic* movement, founded thirty years earlier by Rabbi Yisrael Baal Shem Tov, known as "The Besht" (and the man who was to succeed him as the movement's leader, Rabbi Dov Ber "the Great Magid" of Mezritch). In the wake of the letter, a number of communities issued manifestoes against the new movement, and at the large fairs bans were pronounced on it. The efforts to suppress the movement continued for a whole generation, so that by the end of the eighteenth century, Polish Jewry was split into two camps: *Hasidim* and *Mitnagdim.*

꽃   꽃

In this paper, I shall try to clarify several questions pertaining to the beginnings of the controversy between the *Hasidim* and the *Mitnagdim.*

The first question is: what was the real and important reason that generated the conflict?

We know that most of the charges levelled against the *Hasidim* were not new. There are written testimonies—going back many years before the onset of the public controversy—that speak of groups of people holding their own separate prayer services, of the growing number of people indulging in Kabbalistic practices, and of groups engaging in "ribaldry." The *Derush* literature contains a great deal of criticism of these phenomena. However, the criticism did not yet generate an orgaized public campaign.

Why was it precisely Hasidism that evoked such a reaction?

What special social or spiritual characteristic was the real cause of the conflict, with all the other arguments only serving as supporting elements?

The second question is related to this: who were the initiators and the moving spirits of the attack on *Hasidism*? Why do all the bans and letters contain only the signatures of certain rabbis and not of others? Why are some of them signed by the Gaon of Vilna and members of the *klauz* of Brody who were not rabbis? What was the social force that motivated such an aggressive and determined struggle against *Hasidism*?

The scholars are divided on the answers to these questions. One school of thought maintains that the decisive factor was the emergence of *Hasidism* as a movement that challenged the status of the rabbis and the *parnassim*, communal leaders. Consequently, the latter fought to protect their positions and the entire status quo.

Another theory has it that *Hasidism* challenged the existing scale of spiritual values, placing faith and piety before learning. Therefore, the scholars and rabbis fought to defend the study of Torah and the traditional order of priorities.

These two schools of thought, then, share the view that the *Hasidim* were a rebellious element, while the *Mitnagdim* were Establishment people defending either the social status quo or the traditional spiritual values.

There is another question worth clarifying: why did the controversy erupt only in 1772? The leaders of *Hasidism* had been active for fully a generation and had gained tens of thousands of followers. The movement did not operate clandestinely; on the contrary—its emissaries and preachers travelled all over Poland, speaking, teaching and organizing publicly. Why didn't this activity arouse opposition earlier?

Most scholars say that until 1772 *Hasidism* operated in the remote, backward regions of Podolia and Wolhynia. The Establishment circles were stirred into action against the rebel *Hasidim* only when the latter started spreading in more developed areas, especially after it penetrated into White Russia and Lithuania.

This explanation is also based on the assumption that the *Hasidim* were the rebels while the *Mitnagdim* were the Establishment, and the timing of the clash between them was determined by their relative positions and strengths.

The view that the *Hasidim* and the *Mitnagdim* represented two social and spiritual poles in Jewish society and that the quarrel between them was the result of the contradictions and tension between them is expressed in studies of various aspects of the two groups.

The *Hasidim* are described as originating from oppositionist circles in Jewish society, such as the *"magidim"* and *"mochihim"* (chastizers or rebukers) or "popular *Hasidim*." These circles are also believed to be the authors of the trenchant social criticism found in the *Derush* literature of that period. So *Hasidism* is considered to have sprouted and grown in response to the faults and corruption of organized Jewish communal life and to have included the oppositionist forces.

The *Mitnagdim*, on the other hand, are described as the Establishment people—the rabbis and the *parnassim* who constituted the communal leadership. Many of them signed the anti-*Hasidic* pronouncements—a fact cited in support of the view that the conflict was one between opposition and Establishment.

Spiritually speaking the founders of *Hasidism* are described as *Kabbalists* who preferred tracts on piety and *Mussar*, ethical issues, over *Halacha*, Jewish law, and who ranked *Yir'at shamayim*, religious experience, above scholarship. On the other hand, the *Mitnagdim* are portrayed as *talmidei hachamim*, Talmudic scholars, defending the supremacy of scholarship and erudition.

The link between *Hasidism* and the common people, the movements *Kabbalistic* inclinations, and the geographical area in which it began and first flourished, led some scholars to connect it with the Shabtai Zvi and Frankist movements.

The *Mitnagdim* were portrayed as continuers of the struggle against Sabbatianism, and this factor was cited to explain the intensity of the battle against *Hasidism*.

The answers to these questions that historical research supplies are not new. The image of the *Hasidim* as rebels, as subverters, and the image of the *Mitnagdim* as representatives of the Establishment and the traditional values—these images hark back to the early stages of the public controversy between the two camps.

At the very beginning, the *Mitnagdim* presented themselves as the defenders of Torah and tradition and the *Hasidim* as ignoramuses, hypocrites and subverters of those values. The closeness of the founders of *Hasidism* to the common people and to the simple village *yishuvniks*—the sectors that were regarded as far removed from the leadership of the *kehillah*, the Jewish community—made it easy to pin labels of separatism and subversion on the movement.

The early *Maskilim*, modern Jewish Enlighteners, also played a part in spreading the accepted typology. These *Maskilim*, who were themselves accused of heresy and rebellion and who were attacked mainly by *Hasidim*, sought some connection with the chain of tradition, and they linked themselves with the *Mitnagdim*. In their writings, the *Maskilim* describe Maimonides, the Gaon of Vilna and themselves as part of a rationalistic tradition, while the *Hasidim* are portrayed as benighted Sabbatians.

Thus, the *Maskilim* also had a part in the portrayal of the *Hasidim* and *Mitnagdim* as two ideologically opposing forces in Jewry.

We see, then, that the view that the *Hasidim* and *Mitnagdim* represented two poles in Jewry, from both the social and the spiritual standpoints, prevails both in present-day research and in our cultural tradition. But there are a number of important facts that raise doubts about this view.

Examination of the signatures on the anti-*Hasidic* manifestoes reveals relatively few rabbis and *parnassim* among them. There certainly are not so many as we might expect to find, in light of the assertion that the Jewish leadership and establishment had gone to war to defend their position.

Not too many years earlier Polish Jewry had been shaken by several storms: the Frankist episode and the Eibeschutz-Emden dispute. In both instances groups of Polish rabbis took united stands. The reaction of the Polish rabbis and *Gedolei Torah* to *Hasidism* was much more restrained. With a few exceptions like Rabbi Shlomo of Chelm, Rabbi Haim Rapaport and Rabbi Avraham Katzenellenbogen, their names do not appear in the writings connected with the dispute. Outstanding rabbis and *Gedolei Torah* of that time in fact did not react to the rise of *Hasidism*. This fact raises doubts about the

assertion that the *Mitnagdim* represented the
entire Jewish establishment and leadership.

Another doubt pertains to the bans issued
against *Hasidism*. In the early polemical
writings, the *Hasidic* leaders go virtually
unmentioned. Is it possible that the rabbis and
parnassim of Brody didn't hear about the Baal
Shem Tov or the Magid of Mezritch and their
disciples? Why did they not excommunicate
them by name? Can it be that the rabbis and
parnassim of a large city like Brody were afraid
of some *"baal shem"* (some so-called "master of
the name") in some remote hamlet, or of some
preacher in another hamlet?

Or is it possible that they did not
excommunicate or execrate them because the
so-called Establishment regarded the *Hasidic*
leaders as honored and dear personages rather
than as enemies?   As to the assertions about
Hasidism's Kabbalistic inclinations and the
Maskilim's preference for *Halachah*—scholars
have already pointed out that interest in
Kabbalah and a preference for writings on piety
and *Mussar* were not an innovation of the
Hasidim. They were, in fact, part of a long
process that began many years before the rise of
Hasidism. Interesting testimony to this is
contained in Rabbi Shlomo of Chelm's preface
to his book *Merkevet Hamishneh* published in
1751. Rabbi Shlomo lists various kinds of study
groups in Poland, and from his description and

criticism it is clear that *Mussar* and *Kabbalistic* writings were rated high by most of them.

Questionable, too, is the assertion that the timing of the dispute was influenced by the fact that *Hasidism* developed in the backward regions. The Baal Shem Tov and the Magid of Mezritch operated not far from places like Brody, Lwow, and Zhylkowa, which were centers of Jewish scholarship and leadership in Poland. Miedzibozh itself was a major Chartorisky city, with a population of some two thousand Jews. Can that be regarded as a "remote" place?

Let us assume it can.

Well, twenty years earlier the Frankist movement sprang up in that very area, and leaders of Polish Jewry reacted promptly. Why did they not do the same when the *Hasidim* appeared in the same area.

In view of these doubts, I decided to reexamine the *Hasidic* and *Mitnagdic* views on social and spiritual questions that are regarded as bones of contention. One approach was to examine the positions of those known as *Hasidim* and *Mitnagdim*. Another approach, which proved interesting, was to examine the works of *darshanim*, preachers, and writers of that period who took stands on social and spiritual questions and then try to find out which were *Hasidim* and which *Mitnagdim*.

Both approaches led to interesting findings in both the social and spiritual spheres.

First, the social sphere. Generally speaking, the social criticism in the *Mitnagdic Derush* literature is much broader and more trenchant than that of the *Hasidic* writers. An example of this is the book by Rabbi Hillel ben Z'ev, *Heilel ben Shahar*, which is considered one of the important sources on the decline of the *kehillah*, and the background to the rise of *Hasidism*. Later, this Rabbi Hillel's name appears on a letter sent by disciples of the Vilna Gaon in Eretz Yisrael.

As to the social activities of the *Hasidim* and *Mitnagdim*, it seems that the founders of *Hasidism* were not inclined to criticize the activities of the *kahal* directly. Their social action was limited to spheres in which the authority of the *kehillah* had been weakened or was not clearly defined. Sometimes they also gave their moral sanction to social and institutional norms that had been undermined, such as the well-known episode involving Rabbi Aharon of Karlin, who in the name of his master, the Magid of Mezritch, supported the decisions of the heads of the *kehillah* in a tax-farming matter.

It is rather among the *Mitnagdim* that I have found blatant oppositionists who criticized the operations of the *kehillah* and quarrelled constantly with their leaders over the way they handled the matters under their jurisdiction. These people sometimes accepted communal posts and tried to change things while continuing their struggle against the *parnassim.* One such person was Rabbi Eliahu ben Gershon of Pinczew (Pinchov). In his writings he describes a life of hardship as a result of his struggle against the Establishment, which caused him to be identified as an outstanding representative of what is called opposition. Careful examination of his books reveals that he was a blatant *Mitnaged* and one of the first and sharpest critics of *Hasidism.*

On the *Hasidic* side, there are a number of famous rabbis who are treated with respect in *Mitnagdic* writings at the very height of the dispute. Examples of this are Rabbi Yaacov Yosef of Polnaya and Rabbi Levi Yitzhak of Berditchev, who are called *"Hasida U-perisha,"* an epithet reserved for very special people, and these two are designated thus alongside the Gaon of Vilna.

Hence, the attempt to present the *Hasidim* and *Mitnagdim* as representatives of two diametrically opposed social forces—Establishment and opposition—does not stand up.

I have come to the same conclusion with respect to the spiritual situation. The *Mussar* literature and the *Kabbalah* earned no less attention and appreciation from those we know as *Mitnagdim* than they did from the *Hasidim.* There were differences of opinion over when to study *Kabbalah* and who should be allowed to engage in *Kabbalistic* ways. But this debate cut across the *Hasidic-Mitnagdic* lines.

In fact, in the *Mitnagdic* camp I have found a phenomenon that is usually attributed to the *Hasidim*: the desire to disseminate *Kabbalah* among the general public. Two books for the study of *Kabbalah* written at that time, which explicitly declare an intention to spread *Kabbalistic* knowledge, were written by *Mitnagdim*.

On the other hand, I have found in *Hasidic* writings considerable reservations about the very publication of *Kabbalistic* works. There was even an attempt to restrict the study of *Kabbalah* to the movement's leaders and not to disseminate it among the masses. Clear evidence of this tendency appears in the critical letters sent from Eretz Yisrael by Rabbi Avraham of Kaliska to Rabbi Shneur Zalman of Liadi after the latter's book, *Tanya*, was published.

So in the spiritual field, too, we do not find the *Hasidim* and *Mitnagdim* at opposite poles. Examination of the *Derush* literature from the period of the beginning of *Hasidism* has led me to another conclusion. Not only are the *Hasidim* and *Mitnagdim* not at opposite poles of Jewish society, but among the *Mitnagdim* there is even a group stemming from the same circles as the founders and early leaders of *Hasidim*. To be sure, the *Mitnagdim* include rabbis and *parnassim* belonging to the Establishment and the leadership. But the moving force in the struggle against *Hasidism* is precisely that

element among the *Mitnagdim* who, in their
spirit and in their ways, show an affinity to the
founders of *Hasidism*.

The common social origin of the founders of
Hasidism and the active *Mitnagdim* was the
circle of *"Tzaddikim* and *Hasidim"* that I have
tried to describe in my paper in the journal *Zion*
(Vol. XLVII [1982], 253-292). These were
Mekubbalim and *Perushim*, pietists, who
devoted all their time to the service of God.
They had customs of their own based on
Kabbalah, and a lifestyle of a group that has set
itself apart from the general community
because of its stricter practices with regard to
prayer and *kashrut*. It was a radical circle whose
members were characterized by their
aggressiveness, enthusiasm and firm faith in the
rightness of their way.

What they share in the period of the rise of
Hasidism was an effort to overcome the
alienation, and even hostility, between the
talmidei hachamim—the scholars—and the
masses. That is why they emphasized the
importance of partnership between the learned
person and the common man and described the
nation as an organic body whose different parts
are linked to and dependent on each other.

These groups had a powerful sense of
respnsibility for the situation of *Klal Yisrael* and
a desire to lead the people along the right path,
especially in matters of piety affecting the
general public: *shehitah* (ritual slaughtering),

hazzanut (conducting the prayer service), and the teaching of children.

However, in the framework of these common tendencies, different approaches developed within that camp of *"Tzaddikim* and *Hasidim."* On social and spiritual questions, the early *Hasidic* leaders were full of optimism, permeated with a positive attitude to life and even to the *Galut*, Diaspora living. Others took a pessimistic view and consequently were given to intense Messianic expectations and calculations.

The founding fathers of *Hasidism* created an image of the *Tzaddik* as someone who has power and influence both in Heaven and on earth. The others portrayed the *Tzaddik* as a suffering pauper. The founding fathers of *Hasidism* developed the concept that the *Tzaddik* has to mingle with the masses. The others criticize them and demanded continuation of the tradition of reclusion and solitude.

Both groups wanted to improve Jewish society. The *Hasidim*, for whom gregariousness was a principle, turned to the masses. The others, those who practiced reclusion, tried to improve the nation as a whole by working to improve its institutions.

The *Hasidim* crystallized into a movement. Their spiritual and social outlooks led to a consolidation of ranks, with the masses rallying around the *Tzaddik*. That is how the *Tzaddikim* achieved the leadership status they sought. That, too, is why their social criticism softened. They did not need the *kehilla's* institutions to direct the people; they did so themselves.

What happened to the *perushim* and *mekubbalim* who differed with their colleagues who had become the founding fathers of *Hasidism*? Why didn't they, too, develop into a movement? The main reason for this seems to have been their social views. Their sense of social responsibility caused them to resort to the *kehilla's* institutions. Some of them continued the tradition of *perishut* and tried to influence the institutions from the outside, by guidance or by criticism. Others became rabbis or *dayanim*, religious judges, using their authority to improve the *kehilla*. In the end, they became integrated into the traditional leadership, cooperating with it in strengthening the *kehilla's* authority.

The dispute between *Hasidim* and *Mitnagdim* was not a product of geographical processes in the spread of *Hasidism*. It was linked to the social development of both *Hasidism* and the other group.

The founding fathers of *Hasidism* succeeded in realizing the principle of linking up the *Tzaddik* with the masses and then founded the *Hasidic* community. Their comrades who differed with them came closer to the *kehilla* institutions and even became part of them.

Then there took place in Poland certain political developments that sharpened the differences between the two camps and caused the final rift and the outbreak of the dispute between *Hasidim* and *Mitnagdim*.

The 1760s and 1770s were years of trial for Jewish autonomy in Poland. The dissolution in 1764 of the *"Vaad Arba Ha'aratzot"*—the "Council of the four Lands"—the disintegration of the Polish central government, and the first partition of Poland in 1772 undermined the unity of Polish Jewry and its autonomous leadership.

Under the circumstances, the attitude to the communal institutions and their powers became a central public issue. The *Hasidim*, who had already set up an alternative leadership, were indifferent to the decline of the authority of the traditional institutions. In several areas, they indirectly contributed to this decline—such as when they assumed the authority to appoint *shochtim* (ritual slaughterers) or when the establishment of *Hasidic* minyanim emptied the other synagogues. In certain other areas, however, the *Hasidim* upheld decisions of the *kehilla* institutions and even gave them moral support.

On the other hand, among the *Tzaddikim* and *Hasidim,"* who adopted authoritarian stances, the issue of Jewish autonomy became a central one. The criticism in their books of the *kehilla* institutions is extremely trenchant. This, however, stems from concern and a sense of responsibility, not from hostility or contempt. Precisely in the books containing the most trenchant social criticism, one very often finds expressions of regret over the deterioration of the Jewish autonomy system.

In ordinary circumstances, perhaps, the debate on ideological issues between the founders of *Hasidism* and their comrades would have continued, and the communal leadership would have reconciled itself to the rise of *Hasidism*. Under the circumstances, however, of a period of trial for the traditional Jewish communal leadership setup, the conditions were created for a public struggle between the *Hasidim* and *Mitnagdim*.

The group of *Mekubbalim* and *Perushim* who differed with the founding fathers of *Hasidism* and kept close to the *kehilla* leadership retained the fervor and militancy of the radical circles from which they originated. That is why they became the initiators and driving forces of the communal leadership's struggle against the *Hasidim*. That is why the signatures of the Gaon of Vilna and the *klauz* of Brody appear on the first, and main, anti-*Hasidic* manifestoes.

Study of the paths taken by the *Perushim* and *Mekubbalim* from those circles after the rise of *Hasidism* in the time of the public polemics reveals that they split into two camps. Some became the spearhead of the struggle against the *Hasidim*. This trend is represented by the

Gaon of Vilna, the Magid of Makowa (Makov) and Rabbi Yisrael Leibel.

At the same time, we find people from the same circles who early reconciled with the *Hasidic* leaders. Several members of the Brody *klauz* were the first to mention the *Hasidic* founding fathers in their writings, and they even received *haskamot*—letters of approval—for their books from them.

Among those of the *Perushim* and *Mekubbalim* whose approach was authoritarian and who tried to improve the *kehilla* institutions, there was one who tried to impose his authority on the Establishment but was not swallowed up by it. He was the Gaon of Vilna. For some years he was a lone fighter against both *Hasidism* and the Establishment, and he laid the foundations for *Mitnagdut* as a social and ideological stream. Some of the ideas that originated in the *Perushim* and *Mekubbalim* circles were crystallized in the Vilna Gaon's circles into a new social theory, one that contradicted *Hasidism*.

This perception of the social link between and common origin of the founders of *Hasidism* and *Mitnagdut* helps to explain certain information and traditions we have about some of the leaders of both groups. There is, for example, a tradition about Rabbi David of Makowa (Makov), one of the great foes of *Hasidism*, that he had been a disciple of Rabbi Menahem Mendel of Vitebsk. Rabbi Avraham of Kaliska, a *Hasidic* leader, is said to have been a disciple of the Gaon of Vilna. The early writings of Rabbi Yisrael Leibel, a leading antagonist of *Hasidism* in the 1790s, contain praises of the Magid of Mezritch, who succeeded the Baal Shem Tov as leader of the *Hasidim*. A whole list of books published in the last two decades of the eighteenth century quote *Hasidic* leaders and *Mitnagdim* side by side.

In 1775, the *Hasidic* leaders made an effort to placate the *Mitnagdim*. Two *Hasidic* leaders—Rabbi Menahem Mendel of Vitebsk and Rabbi Shneur Zalman of Liadi—sought authoritative sanction for this step. They did not apply to the established communal leaders and rabbis. They went to the Gaon of Vilna. In the last analysis, they regarded their great foe as the true authority. In spite of his hatred, he was one of them.

MAHARAL AND EARLY HASIDISM
Bezalel Safran

Preface

Awareness of the affinity between Hasidic teaching and that of R. Judah Loew (Maharal) of Prague is not new. Two Hasidic masters of the nineteenth century—Rabbi Israel of Kozhnitz and Rabbi Mendel of Kotzk—made the Maharal's works required reading for their followers.[1] Twentieth-century historical scholarship has also not overlooked the similarity between some ideas of the sixteenth-century rabbi and mystic and those of early Hasidism. G. Scholem has alluded to the relation in a general way.[2] Gottesdiener has noted adumbration of the Hasidic Zaddik in R. Judah Loew's work;[3] Sherwin pointed to the roots of Hasidic *devekut* in the Maharal's works.[4]

This article will pursue the relation between R. Judah Loew and early Hasidism further and will attempt to prove: (a) that the former was a major intellectual influence on the new movement, as exemplified in the works of R. Menahem Mendel of Vitebsk, a leading theoretician as well as organizer of early Hasidism,[5] and (b) that sensitivity to the Maharal's thought system provides an important—perhaps indispensable —context for understanding early Hasidic teaching.

In establishing a relation between Maharal and early Hasidic teaching, we will be looking for unique themes shared by Maharal and R. Menahem Mendel as well as terms and exegetical topoi coined by Maharal which are appropriated by the Hasidic writer. But beyond these specific issues, it will be shown that the two writers under consideration communicate within a common universe of discourse, with identical premises underlying their spiritual concerns.

A major problem in understanding Maharal's writing is accounting for what frequently appears as vagueness of formulation, fragmented presentation and repetition. The reader is tantalized by the suggestive hints but often finds it difficult to grasp the core.

Maharal's "impervious" meaning seems to have posed a problem even to readers who discerned its general Hasidic intent. Followers of R. Mendel of Kotzk complained of Maharal's redundancy; he himself, however, reprimanded them, considering Maharal to be a precise writer, and his repetitions only apparent.[6]

This study will attempt to read Maharal as a precise writer: to ascertain the meaning of particular aspects of his thought by determining the sense of recurrent key terms and by collating his scattered fragments.[7] When this is accomplished, the relation of these to the thought of R. Mendel of Vitebsk will be explored.

Part I

A pivotal term in Maharal's writing, frequently employed, is *yosher*, integrity. *Derek yosher*, the way of integrity, is the goal toward which his ethical theory gravitates.[1] It is employed synonymously with *derek hayim*,[2] way of life—the title of Maharal's most thorough presentation of his views—as well as with *miẓu'a* (the mean), *shivuy* (balance), and *devekut*[3] (communion with God), all of which are identified explicitly with the ideal state. Determining the meanings of this term—and those it entails—will greatly facilitate our understanding of Maharal's ethical works.

In the course of commenting on a statement by R. Joshua (Avot 2:12) on how hatred of other people "takes one out of the world," Maharal highlights two themes:[4]

First, resentment of others is gratuitous, since it is essentially resentment of one's self. Secondly, the resentment of self stems from an inability to reconcile one's self to one's own faults. A whole person, *adam shalem*, would be reconciled to lapses and would not need to project resentment onto others.[5] The term *shalem* then does not signify perfection; it connotes self-acceptance.[6] It is in this way that *adam shalem* exhibits integrity:[7] to resent others —who are a mirror of one's self—is to be antagonistic to one's self, and hence, to deviate from *yosher*, which constitutes the ideal state.[8]

It follows that a judgmental stance vis-à-vis others is precarious. One would be prone to be critical of others precisely where one failed, so that censure of others is really censure of self; self-judgment should therefore precede evaluation of others.[9] The Noahide law concerning the establishment of a system of justice is interpreted negatively[10]—it entails shunning judgment of others. In judging others the *yosher* is violated which should exist inwardly, i.e., the state of reconciliation to one's own shortcomings, which others simply bring into consciousness.[11]

That judgment of others is linked with one's own integrity, *yosher*, was developed by Maharal elsewhere.[12] In his aforementioned comment on the meaning of justice in the Noahide laws, he provides another perspective on *yosher*; it inheres only in the "rational" soul *(nefesh siklit).*[13]

A recurrent dichotomy in Maharal's writings is that between nature, *tev'a,* and the higher reason, *sekel.* There are two orders existing simultaneously in reality, the natural and the supernatural [*sikli* or *nivdal.*][14] Which order, *seder,* one is oriented by is a matter of choice. To be oriented by the order of the natural world, one simply follows one's natural or commonsensical inclination. However, given adequate preparation,[15] one can connect with a non-natural, *sikli*, realm. This can be accomplished by behaving "unnaturally" oneself, i.e., by resisting the "material" tendencies of human nature *(tev'a* or *homer)* which, for example, incline one to judgment of others.[16] It is preferable to focus on the meta-physical, *sikli*, dimension of the encounter with a person who is lacking and hence provokes a judgmental stance. In such a provocative encounter, what is called for primarily for the *nefesh siklit* anchored in *yosher*, is acquiescence in the will of God, who is calling attention to one's own shortcomings through this meeting.[17]

Perceptible reality is only a cover for a deeper reality which reflects a special divine order and with which the "whole" person may connect. This is a crucial premise for Maharal, and its implications are far-reaching. God does not simply exist; He encompasses, *kolel*, all, and there is nothing but Him.[18] This panentheism does not exhaust itself as a theological doctrine; it entails a correlative ethic.[19]

The idea that man was created in the "image of God," *be-zalmo*, is a pervasive one for Maharal[20] and is understood in several senses. The first of these is that it refers to the created world, which is a reflection of the divine.[21] To say that man was created in the image of God is to mean that he was thrust into a reality which is a cover for the divine. *"Be-zalmo"* means within the reality which is His image. The ethical implications are clear: everything one encounters is an image of God. One should therefore not relate to the perceptible image but to the divine image reflected in an experience.

The experience which Maharal dwells on most frequently is an irritating interpersonal relationship. One should defer to a fellow person even if he be provocative; that person is, after all, an "image of God," and, if one connects to the other reality, the *sikli* or *nivdal* dimension, there is an underlying order and meaning in the encounter. [22] By reconciling one's self to a divine message in the encounter, experienced in acquiescence, one resists the pull of human nature and works towards a connection with the divine dimension. There is no need to decode a specific communication in the meeting; it is essentially an impetus to relate to the divine in humility. Maharal's interpretation of a Rabbinic account in the Babylonian Talmud (*Gittin* 7a) may serve as illustration of this point. [23] Mar Ukba sent for advice to R. Eleazar saying: "Certain men are annoying me, and I am able to get them into trouble with the government; shall I do so?" Instructed to restrain himself "even while the wicked are before him," Mar Ukba insisted the situation was intolerable. He was once again advised to restrain himself in the face of God and hope for relief, which came immediately.

Maharal cites this passage in *Netiv ha-Bitahon*[24] and considers it an example of a

"struggle for the sake of the Lord." Faced with
a pressing mundane image of acute annoyance,
Mar Ukba struggles—successfully—to strip the
experience of its natural, "realistic" trappings
and convert it into an image of the divine. The
vigorous, strenuous mental effort entailed in
insisting that confronting him is not the trou-
blemaker, who is only an agent, but rather his
Sender, resulted in the relief from Mar Ukba's
woes.[25] In an analogous context, this effort is
viewed as the core of *devekut*, and it implies a
transcendence of mundane pressures, even as
one cleaves to the divine instead. It is the capacity not to reify, not to "accord reality" to dis-
concerting perceptions, to relate them rather as
divine images.[26]

By experiencing fellow people as messengers
of the divine, one achieves the "image of
God,"[27] understood here as a divine endowment (not as a reality into which one is
thrust—the first meaning, discussed above) but
in the sense of a personal endowment. The
"image of God" is not an innate gift; it is
achieved as a result of the effort of living in
devekut, in communion with God.[28] Deriving
from a divine realm, a transcendent world,[29]
"the next world,"[30] it facilitates the effort of a
person wishing to relate to the transcendent
dimension of a situation in this world, not its
ostensibly natural one. The "image of God," in
this sense, is a radiance, a spark rooted in the
divine light. [31]

This radiance manifests itself on the "heel" of an Adam or Jacob—rather than their face—for the heel is evocative of their ultimate humility,[32] their being reconciled to the humbling trials God sent.[33] Jacob is frequently referred to as exemplifying the ideal state. Two of his names, *Ya'akov* and *Yeshurun*, generate associations of meaning which Maharal employs to unravel his ethical theory. While *Ya'akov* suggests implications of "heel" in the sense just mentioned,[34] *Yeshurun* implies *yosher* in the sense of being reconciled.[35] Both of these converge in Maharal's understanding of Jacob as Truth.

Midrash and Kabbalah view Jacob as paradigmatic of truthfulness, and Maharal often alludes to this identification.[36] Commenting on the Rabbinic statement that there was no illness or sense of weakness prior to the time of Jacob, Maharal suggests that the novelty was in how frailty was experienced by Jacob. His very illness made Jacob discover the Truth which upheld him in his dire straits. The fact that he was able to endure, even in the face of overwhelming weakness, indicated to him that there was something "True" supporting his insupportable being.[37]

Jacob's experience is so crucial to Maharal's understanding of the religious frame of mind that it is invoked as a general principle: the cogency of inferring truth from its opposite.[38] Maharal speaks of a state of utter existential attrition which he calls "nominal death"; expe-

rienced without resentment, it sensitizes one to
the fact of divine sustenance of which one is a
recipient and to its Source. Divine supportiveness is implied by its apparent negation.[39] How
else could one carry on in such excruciating
circumstances if not for the *kiyum*, sustenance,
provided by the divine? In fact, the use of the
term *Makom* as a reference to God is based on
recognition of the divine as sustainer.[40]

A concise summary of the orientation which
has emerged thus far is presented in a comment
on Hillel's ideas about humility in Avot 1:12.[41]

והנה כל אשר הוא עושה עצמו **מקבל** שהוא **משפיל** עצמו
ראוי הוא לקבל החיים מן השי׳ת...כי אל החיים ראוי
הקבלה, שצריך שיהיה מקבל החיות אשר השי׳ת משפיע
תמיד לאדם, **ואין האדם מקוים בו יתברך.** ועצם החיות
בעצמו הוא הקבלה שמקבל חיות, ולפיכך השי׳ת נקרא
מקור חיים...ולפיכך כל אשר הוא משפיל עצמו הוא מקבל
הקיום מן השי׳ י אשר **בו נתלה הכל.**

Effectively evoked in this highly compressed
and "tight" passage is the causal nexus between
kabbalah (receiving) and *kiyum* or *ḥiyut*, divine
sustenance. What is striking at first glance is the
equation between *kabbalah* and *shiflut*, acquiescence. In general, the term *kabbalah*, receiving,
suggests to Maharal precisely that mental attitude of reconciling one's self to God's will,
which provides access to the effluence of the
divine. Hence, the Rabbinic directive—*hevei
kauveil ve-kayyam* (*Sanhedrin* 14a)—is interpreted to mean: be acquiescent in the face of
provocation *(kauveil)* so that you may be quali-

fied to receive divine sustenance, *kiyyum*.[42] That the divine will is expressed through acts of people—sometimes provocative—is the theme of several passages in *Derek Hayim*.[43]

But Maharal does not simply point to the indispensable link between *kabbalah*, acquiescence, and experience of the divine.[44] He also suggests a near-simultaneity of experiencing one's helplessness, even as one is "raised" by the divine revitalizing. One must be affected by the sting of failure in order to experience the divine breath.[45] It is one's "not being," *ayin*, one's "heel," which savors the divine resuscitation. In the same vein, he goes on to suggest that the divine is experienced as a "receiving" of divine support—in acquiescensce.[46]

The term *ayin* to describe "not being" as a result of fright or failure was coined by Maharal.[47] Earlier Kabbalistic usage sees *ayin* as identical with the highest emanation of *Keter*.[48] For Maharal, the word implies an existential state as well. Experiencing one's *ayin* without resentment or despair, relating one's anger or fear to the Source of these emotions, eventually results in experiencing the divine.[49] Anxiety, or fear in general, consists in perceiving one's self as "caused" or being "acted upon," and consequently feeling "as if one is not." The "fearer of God" has this very experience—but relates it to his Cause. As a result, one is completely "with the divine."[50] Being with God, one draws sustenance from Him.[51] If, however, one interprets irritation as determined by mundane causes, which one resents, contact with the Divine—the real Cause—is loosened, as one slips out of the special providential order of *devekut*, communion with God.[52] The divine sustenance which can be received only in relating "stress" to the Source, would be lost by reacting resentfully to provocation.[53] It is only by struggling to stay in a state of *yosher* that *devekut* can be maintained. How else can one expect to be in the special "world" one resides in, in the unique "reality" which one inhabits?[54]

Maharal's account of the religious life is dialectical. While *yosher* (and concomitant terms) are the focal point, the "high" (more precisely, the low) point cannot be sustained indefinitely. The assaults of human nature on the ideal state of *devekut* are constant, and even after the "image of God" is achieved, there may be lapses.[55] Deviation from the state of *yosher* may be triggered from either "right" or "left." These two terms are employed in many parts of the Maharal's work in relation to the ideal state, and in order to arrive at a generalized meaning, it is necessary to collate all usages and abstract their intent.

Already in the programmatic Introduction to *Derek Hayim*, we review what is by now a familiar theme, but with an additional nuance.[56] Walking the "way of *yosher*" is identified with the "way of life," and it entails staying on course, not deviating to "right" or "left."

"Life" is understood as connection with the "tree of life," with the "living God who is Himself eternal life." Such "life" is the content of the experience of *devekut*,[57] and its antithesis is gravitating to "death."[58] The suggestion that there is an identity between "right and left" digressions and "death" is made explicit elsewhere in *Derek Hayim*, particularly in the comment on R. Joshua's statement (*Avot* 2:11), that three traits are responsible for "driving a person out of the world."[59] In other comments, the two digressions, extremes, are invariably identified with "right" and "left."[60]

The larger context of R. Joshua's statement (*Avot* 2:8-2:14) is a group of *mishnayot* which Maharal treats as one thematic unit.[61] This section contains an appreciation of the moral and intellectual virtues of the five students of R. Yohanan ben Zakkai, their particular notions of the "good" way to which one should cleave, and a three-tiered statement by each one, epitomizing this moral tendency. Maharal's evaluation of the five, both individually and collectively, evolves into his most important statement about the relationship among psychology, ethics and the possibility of *devekut*. Emerging from this unit are thought structures which serve him in good stead elsewhere. Relevant to our present concern is his interpretation of the three-tiered teachings as attempts to correct excesses from the right and left in order to reach the "third," ideal state. The meaning of *yosher* was already abstracted from this central unit, and it will be amplified by related passages in the course of the discussion.

Maharal's comment on R. Joshua's statement (*Avor* 2:11)[62] is an attempt to discern "good" from "evil"; in other words, to differentiate the deviations right and left, "evil," from the ideal state, which is evoked as the "good." Maharal is about to express his ideas in a new context. As he varies his terminology, he also introduces new nuances.[63]

The "good," he says, endows creatures with their sustenance, *kiyum*; without it, they would have no "reality." Maharal refers to his fuller discussion of the issue in the first chapter of *Derek Hayim*[64] where two basic points emerge. First, the raison d'être of creation is the "good" that it produces. Secondly, once created, creation draws its sustenance from that "good." Futhermore, there is stress here that a creature must be "good" in itself; and a prooftext: the verse accompanying each facet of creation, "and God saw that it was good," indicates that sustenance, *kiyum*, is possible only because of the "good."

Two questions arise. Does this discussion apply to man? How does Maharal define the "good"? If we wish to conjecture the meaning at this point, there is one hint. The term *kiyum* is recalled from the discussion of *yosher*, and we anticipate that the "good" has an important bearing on it.

Maharal follows up on the relevance of "good" to man,[65] explaining that man does not immediately assume the "goodness" of the rest of creation—he is created lacking—which is why the Creator does not at first perceive him as a "good" creature. When he ultimately attains "goodness," he needs to be "good in himself." What the nature of this "goodness" is is only intimated.[66]

When Maharal's discussion in *Derek Hayim* is correlated with the *Sermon for Shabbat ha-Gadol*, the meaning of man's "goodness" becomes clear.[67] Maharal there explores the situation of man as totally dependent on divine grace, a situation which leads him to *devekut*. In a state of utter dependence

> man is called *mah,* "what [am I?]." From this perspective, nothing inheres in him, and [upon acknowledging this "nothingness"] the divine dwells in man, because he is humble. From the perspective of the divine dwelling in him, however, man is *me'od*, very powerful...since the divine presence elevates his lowliness and renders him mighty, for all is from God. This is what the human situation is about when man understands his state: he is *mah* in himself, and *me'od* as a result of God's mighty, exalted presence.

It is clear from this citation that *me'od* is a precise term. It refers to the endowment of an otherwise lacking being, *mah*, with great worth, *me'od.* Recalling the passage from *Derek Hayim,*[68] we realize that *me'od* is to be equated with "goodness," and Maharal there says in effect that the "good" can inhere only in a person who is aware of his total dependence, *mah.* It is only then that he is "good in himself." In the Sermon, a sense of *mah* is concomitant with Adam's fall; his "return" was rooted in his being reconciled to his dependence.[69] In *Derek Hayim* the link between *mah* and "goodness" is especially poignant because the standard of "goodness" which one ultimately attains is comparable to the "good" state of the rest of creation. They are "good" in themselves because they are committed exclusively to divine service and do not swerve therefrom.[70]

We noticed earlier Maharal's correlation of "truth" and *yosher*, and then of *yosher* and "goodness." Remarkable here is the Maharal's similarity to Naḥmanides' idea, who also views the ideal of "goodness" in terms of the universe which, lacking free will before Adam's fall, is absolutely committed to divine service. Naḥmanides' ethical ideal is a return to a state in which *devekut* is once again absolute, in order for one to be open to the divine fulness.[71] The same Talmudic passage (*Sanhedrin* 42a)—and the benediction which it contains—are employed by both Naḥmanides and Maharal[72] for the intimation of this *devekut* ideal.

When, going back to the comment on R. Joshua's statement (*Avot* 2:11),[73] Maharal speaks of the three elements that drive one out of the "world" (evil "eye," evil urge, hatred of others), he goes on to explain: "When God created His world, He wrote *(katav)* concerning every single one ['and God saw that] it was good'; however, these three traits are 'evil,' the reversal of God's creation."[74] Maharal's explanation is jarring. The Biblical account does *not* indicate that "every single one" *(kol ehad v'ehad)* was good: divine approbation, as Maharal noted in aforementioned passages, was absent after man's creation. The usage of *olam*, world, then, both in the *Avot* passage and in Maharal's allusion to the creation of man, relates once again to the special order of *devekut*. The "good" is the divine sustenance, *kiyum*, which nourishes one in this special order. In fact "wrote *(katav)* concerning everyone...good," may allude to *katav* in the sense which Maharal elucidates in a different context; and it refers to being "hollowed out," just as the tablets were, in order to make room *(miktav)* for the divine "letters" *(k'tav)*.[75] *K'tav* then intimates the state of *mah*.

With a clearer understanding of how the "good" permeates a state of *mah*, the three "traits" can now be accounted for as "evil" distractions from the "good." We may now revert to Maharal's cue that these three traits constitute aberrations right and left from the center of *devekut*, the "good,"[76] aberrations of *guf* and *nefesh*.

The distinction between the terms *guf,* body, and *nefesh,* soul, as used by Maharal, has to do less with the distinction between physical and emotional than with foci, or directions, of a personality. In general, *guf* refers to self-seeking impulses;[77] *nefesh* to other-directed ones.[78] *Guf* has to do with needs and impulses which bring gratification to the self—nutrition, feelings of love, a sense of self-satisfaction.[79] Generically, this whole "right" side is termed *'ervah,*[80] eros, and its close connection with the motive of self-love is suggested.[81] The "left side" is reactive in that it is both provoked by and affects others. Envy, anger and hatred are some of the "sinister" impulses which are aroused by others[82] and, if given their way, will bring harm to them. This side is characterized by a certain hardness and obstinacy.[83]

Some of the graphic dichotomies which Maharal suggestively employs for the sides of right and left, respectively, are lion and serpent, water and fire, heat and cold, love and fear.[84] These digressions, "extremes," are to be avoided. They are the *yezer ha-ra,* the "evil" inclinations,[85] their motive force is pride, [86] and they are often equated with the "self."[87] When not expressly used in contradistinction to each other, *guf* and *nefesh* are both considered "material" and may be used interchangeably with other terms for matter, *geshem* and *homer.* As such, they share a common trait. Matter is *mitpa'el,* subject to fluctuation and change.[88]

Guilt, for example, which implies fluctuation, is a "material" impulse, not conducive to attainment of the ideal state.[89]

How to move from digressions "right and left" to the state of *yosher*—and how to struggle to remain there once arrived—may be illustrated by Maharal's discussion of love and fear, water and fire and R. Yohanan ben Zakkai's disciples' notions of *devekut*.

We have seen earlier that resentment of others—a "left" emotion—mirrors resentment of self and is viewed in contrast to *kiyum* of the true "reality."[90] This inner "baggage" surfacing from the left emerges even more clearly in the discussion of fear. Fear (as typical of other leftward emotions) does not inhere in reality, but in morose reflection upon reality. The fear is in one's self, in one's perception of a situation and, if not checked, would be self-fulfilling. Maharal elaborates this notion.[91]

> Whoever persistently fears something ultimately comes to experience the fear as reality....When he persistently fears poverty, he attains poverty in actuality. "That which I feared will overcome me" (Job 3:25) alludes to a situation when he fears something and is inclined to surrender to that which he fears. He thereby "accepts" that which he fears....When he "gives himself" to [fear] of this privation, he "receives" the privation which pursues him.

Key phrases in this passage suggest the state of mind in which fear is transposed into reality. One "gives one's self" over to the perceived privation and mentally confirms the fearsome reality which haunts one ("receives" it). These impulses come naturally for the self, for "one is inclined to surrender to that which one fears."

Fear is offset by *bitahon*, trust: it is precisely these natural indulgences[92] that a trust in God struggles to override. *Bitahon* is a quest to reach beyond a perceived reality into a realm where the bleak perception is overcome and a favorable reality takes its place.[93]

This secure realm is a reflection of "Torah," interpreted here in a special sense. The phrase, "to work at Torah,"[94] is understood as fortifying the meta-natural order, *sikli*, over the natural impulses, *ḥomer*.[95] Torah itself is identified with the transcendent order of reality, above and beyond natural reality.[96]

In the course of explaining this notion of Torah, Maharal juxtaposes two contrasting instances of how a mental frame can shape reality.[97] The first is a fear of falling which produces a fall.[98] The second concerns being "engaged with Torah" in the sense just mentioned, overwhelming natural impulses and fears by reaching out for the transcendent order of Torah, "beyond time,"[99] where faith turns into an actual reality.

This "reaching out" is strenuous, for it requires a denial of one's perceptions.[100] If suc-

cumbing to one's fears entails mentally accept-
ing a fearful prospect, commitment to the
transcendent order of Torah and *bitahon* pre-
sume a mental struggle against it.[101]

Two Rabbinic statements, that "all is in the
hands of heaven except for the fear of
heaven"[102] and "all is in the hands of heaven
except for cold and heat"[103] provide a context
for discussing the relationship between self-
inspired fear and fear of heaven.[104] Heat and
cold, we recall, are employed by Maharal to
evoke the right-left dichotomy. Cold is used to
suggest fear and is associated with the left, just
as heat suggests self-love and "rightward"
impulses. To say that fear (cold) is not in the
"hand of heaven" indicates that fear, or love
(heat), interpose between event and religious
response. A person, being reflective, *mitpa'el*,
interprets a situation frightfully, thereby setting
up intermediaries—*emza'im*—between it and
the divine. Rather, one should choose immediately to transpose one's fear into "fear of
heaven" by relating it to its ultimate cause, *'ila*,
thereby placing one's self in the "hands of
heaven."[105]

The statement "fear of heaven is not in the
hands of heaven" is thus in tension with the one
concerning "heat and cold," i.e., love and fear.
Which will prevail depends on personal choice,
on whether one will indulge reflexive fears, or
rise for a struggle to convert anxiety into fear of
heaven, by arresting the anxiety. When the lat-

ter course is opted for, one is drawn into heaven's domain, beyond danger.[106]

Free will is meaningful precisely in such straits, as Maharal suggests in *Derek Hayim*.[107] Out of Eden, but endowed with the image of God, one may choose to relate stimuli or irritants in the world of experience to their ultimate cause, *litlot ba-'ilah*, and to rise above them, or to remain "locked" into the phenomenal world.[108] In Eden, the former course came naturally;[109] now it requires a choice—not a theoretical assent, a mere belief in the existence of a transcendent realm: but, in effect, a decision to relate the fear.[110] The arrested anxiety merges into a "fear of heaven."[111]

Not to struggle to arrest the fear, to "reify" an anxious perception of reality, is idolatrous, and this meaning of the worship of foreign gods, *'avodah zarah*, is consistently and effectively employed by Maharal. Indeed, the right-left dichotomy is also expressed as tendencies of two evil urges: forbidden love, *'ervah*, on the right, and idolatry, *'avodah zarah*, on the left.[112] To react to the "realistic" dimension of a provocation by a fellow person or an irritating natural phenomenon is "idolatrous" because it misses the potential for a relationship to the divine, latent in such encounters.[113]

Feelings of love or "right" impulses, too, need to be related to the Source. The complex of emotions mentioned earlier under the rubric of *guf*, evoked by the symbolism of heat and water, motivated by self-love, are stimuli which the "whole" person stills, so that religious sevice is linked to the divine only.

Maharal explains why, at the time of meeting his long-lost Joseph, Jacob was concentrating on "Shema." Underlying his account is the premise that the deep love felt for Joseph was restrained for the sake of heaven, and thereby related to the divine.[114] Other deep feelings one experiences are transferred heavenward in the same way.[115]

Maharal frequently suggests that consciousness of one's successful ethical achievement vitiates the potential of *devekut*. Dwelling on an accomplishment results in complacency (the "right" motive of self-satisfaction) and a fall. One is never actually "complete," yet must always gravitate[116] toward that state, "always be about to be whole."[116] But the state of *shlemut* (wholeness) harbors *yezer ha-ra* and will precipitate a "fall." The sense of being whole must therefore be fought.[117] Esau, who has already "achieved" peace and completeness, is viewed in contradistinction to Jacob, who is still aiming for it, making his way *(dorek)* towards *shlemut*.[118]

Commenting on a Talmudic statement attributed to Rabbi Jose[119]—"may my portion be with those who die on the way to the performance of a religious duty"—Maharal asks why Rabbi Jose does not want to share with those who actually accomplish their religious intention. He suggests that "moving toward" God makes it possible to be with Him, but consummating an achievement necessarily results in self-satisfaction and alienates from the divine rather than drawing one closer. "Dying," or arresting the sense of self-achievement, on the way to a mitzvah, which holds out the promise of selfless *devekut*, is therefore ideal.[120]

It is at this point that the "third" or "middle" ground between left and right becomes relevant. References have already been made to Maharal's comment on *Avot* 2:12, R. Joshua's statement on the three traits. R. Joshua is one of five students of R. Yohanan ben Zakkai, and in each of their teachings Maharal finds such "middle" ground between the poles where *yosher* is allowed to take root.[121]

For example, R. Eliezer ben Horkenos teaches deference to a fellow person so that one can become privy to the "world-to-come," an appeal concerning a "right" impulse; an admonition to restrain anger, a control of the "left." The third advice concerns one's situation after a lapse or failure, for which the counsel is: "return [to God] one day before your death."[122]

Return, *t'shuva*, consists in realizing one is *mah* as a result of failure.[123] A lack, or sin, is precipitated as a result of pride[124] and "return" therefore involves a humble concession that one is in need of ongoing divine assistance through "causes"[125] to help one refrain from falling.[126] David's fall and return are paradigmatic of this

mode of return.[127] The fall was necessitated by
the divine as a result of David's sense of moral
self-sufficiency verbalized as "test and try me"
(*Psalms* 26:2).[128] "Return" therefore consisted
in acknowledging the divine as the Source
which makes virtue possible.[129] The ultimate
purpose of David's fall and return was to teach
this very idea: David's "return" is paradigmatic
for all.[130]

In light of these considerations, the teaching
"return...before your 'death'" is understood as
follows. Facilitating a return to the "middle,"
to *yosher*, is an effort to do so immediately,
before the onset of "death."[131] Death, we recall,
is used in the sense of distraction from "good"
or "life":[132] guilt is viewed by Maharal as such
an aberration from being reconciled in *yosher*.

Guilt is a "material" impulse, it smacks of the
poles, of the "extremes," and obscures a
genuine return.[133] Return means being reconciled to one's failure, in acknowledgment,
hoda'a, of total dependence on the divine—
without the distraction of guilt.[134] "Matter"
implies repentance based on guilt, in which the
people of Nineveh also shared. "Form," on the
other hand, is "return," in the sense of return to
the Source in total dependence; and it requires
obstinate perseverance to resist the "material"
poles which are self-centered, in order to stay
with the divine.[135]

The struggle for *devekut*, or *yosher*, from the
"fires" of failure, is also evoked by the imagery

of rising from the "fire" of guilt to the "fire" or Torah. That Torah was given to Israel because they are bold faced, a Rabbinic statement, is understood precisely in this sense. Boldness and obstinacy, "left" traits, are valuable in insuring perseverance towards the transcendent "order" of Torah—likened to fire—from the "hell" of failure, also likened to fire.[136] The other three-tiered teachings of R. Yohanan ben Zakkai's disciples are interpreted analogously, i.e., the third component concerns the situation after a fall, which one "elevates." One more example will clinch the point.

When R. Joshua speaks of the "enmity of others" as the third trait drawing one away from the world of *devekut,*[137] he viewed the situation in which such enmity might occur as a crossroads. If one stumbles into envy or anger (i.e., the content, as Maharal understands it, of the second trait which "takes one out of the world," evil eye), one may either project the guilt at the root of one's anger[138] onto others, as "enmity of others,"[139] or one may arrest this projection.[140] If one opts for the latter, *yosher* is attained.

Moving from "evil" to "good" is a dialectical process. For if the two foci of "evil" in human character—"right and left"—are burdened by perceptions of self which are not conducive to divine service, how will one arrive at the "good" which is purged of these perceptions? The answer is couched in different modes, but its

underlying message is consistent: a human gesture towards the "good" is realized as an
achievement of the divine, not of man.

The realm of "good," on the one hand, and
"evil" distractions from the "extremes," on the
other, are contradictory.[141] To bridge them
requires a supernatural feat. Only the divine can
override the "law of contradiction" to achieve
the "good" service—pursued for the sake of
heaven.[142] A "controversy for the sake of
heaven" is understood in this sense. The
"parts"[143] of *guf* and *nefesh* may transcend their
self-centered origins and be related for the sake
of heaven only through divine sustenance,
kiyum.[144] Only the divine who joins irreconcila-
ble opposites (the realm of unity, on the one
hand, and the "parts," on the other) makes the
relating of human fears—and loves—"for the
sake of heaven" possible.[145]

With this understanding as background, a
phrase cited earlier[146] should be viewed more
comprehensively. Maharal's link of *yosher* with
the divine,[147] as well as his pervasive usage of
'azmo as the self, a resultant of "right" and
"left" impulses, *prima facie* contradicts a previously cited phrase, "resentment of others is a
digression from one's self, which is *yosher.*[148] Is
the self an expression of alienation from *devekut*
or is it *yosher*?

The self's perceptions (through "right-left"
filters) of others' faults are aberrations from the
ideal; the ideal calls for restraint and "relating"

in the face of provocation.[149] If such a response of "reconciliation to the divine,"[150] rather than enmity, is indeed achieved, that must be the work of the divine elevating the self; "He, blessed be He, is the *yosher* in the self."[151] Given the nature of man as he is in himself, [152] one's preponderance towards evil,[153] how else could the "digressions" have been arrested?

Maharal's pessimistic view of human nature, on the one hand, and his conviction that it is God's power that can overcome the *yeẓer ha-ra*, on the other, are given articulate expression in this statement:[154]

> Certainly, man must resist the *yeẓer ha-ra* with all his might but should not imagine that he can oppose it or withstand it. He should rather imagine that [this undertaking] is a very, very difficult thing...and that successful eradication of the *yeẓer* is achieved through God, for it is He who removes the *yeẓer ha-ra*. Man, however, as long as he maintains that he can oppose and overcome the *yeẓer* by himself, will rather be overwhelmed by its might.

🙟   🙝

For Maharal, then, the term *yosher* is employed to suggest several perspectives. It epitomizes a "way," *derek yosher*, training one's self to be reconciled, unresenting of being completely dependent on the "good." It points to a goal: sensing the divine "giving" in an experience of *devekut*. Finally, it suggests that the effort of *yosher* in itself is sustained by the divine.

Part II

The transition from Maharal's universe to that of R. Menachem Mendel of Vitebsk is smooth and natural. R. Mendel easily assimilates Maharal's terminology and thought structures as he proceeds to relate them to the teaching of the Baal Shem Tov. He explicitly cites Maharal's *Derek Hayim* as his source for central notions about *devekut*. "Life" is the content of the *devekut* experience and "good" is its source of vitality,[1] ideas whose content in Maharal's commentary on *Avot* have already been quoted at length.[2]

Revealing is not only the fact of citation but also the mode of doing so. Most other titles cited in R. Mendel's works are preceded by the words "in the book."[3] In Maharal's case, such formalism is dropped and the phrase reads simply: והוא הנקרא טוב בדרך החיים.[4] Such citation fuses the work's title and the "way of life" into one whole and bespeaks the familiarity and congeniality of the material. This would explain why the conceptual framework we encountered in Maharal's system and the concomitant terminology are important premises of R. Mendel's comments.

❧   ☙

The focal point of R. Mendel's work is epitomized in this directive:[5] "Worship in inno-

cence without any digression (פנידה)"; this means
a struggle for the awareness that "everything is
from the Creator, and there is nothing in the
world besides Him, as it is said, there is nothing
but You." Prior to Adam's Fall, divine reality
was not disguised so that every occurrence was
obviously, of itself, related to the Source;[6] after-
wards it is a person's duty to strip the veneer of
"nature"[7] and relate an experience to its divine
root, "to find Him who rides in everything."[8]
"God made everything so that He would be
feared" (Eccl. 3:14), and fear of heaven in this
sense is a pervasive theme in R. Mendel's writing.[9] It entails relating anxieties provoked by
events to the core from which they emanate.
One should aim to move from Jacob's heel,
muddled at the bottom,[10] straight to God,[11] a
goal which is achieved by ascent to the Source,
focusing on the "head,"[12] the Cause, [13] rather
than the mundane effect.

Illusory fear is God's way of teaching a person how to come close to Him. Those who
ignore the lesson are preoccupied with perceived reality, instead of Him who vitalizes it.[14]

"Elevating" the fear by relating it heavenward "sweetens" the severe judgment and
allows relief and grace to fill the situation,[15] instead of resentment or fright. For in returning
to the ultimate cause which pervades everything
—persevering to experience *it*, rather than mundane fear—one reaches a world of freedom.[16]
One is then beyond the pale of mundane events,

beyond the reach of harm.[17] Perception of trouble is a function of living in fragmented reality, but above—in the sphere of *devekut*—all is unity. Because of the obfuscating effect of living camouflaged by "nature," one must transfer to the realm beyond.[18] Indeed, the restored, unified reality (עולם התיקון) is already here; it is only the *person* who is "broken," and in a "broken" state, one creates divisiveness.[19] But in struggling to resist "matter," a person comes closer to the divine and realizes that all is unity.[20]

This awareness emerges from a sense that, though it is possible to shake off the fearsome reality, it cannot be done without God's support.[21] Even in the "abyss" there is a "rope" being offered to bail one out, if only despair is fought off:[22] one will recognize that God's dominion extends even to the darkest of spots and that the successful "fight," too, was a divine gift. If, however, the extended hand was not grasped and, instead, one "fell into anger" and permitted natural mechanisms to take over, the rope is severed, and the opportunity to experience God's presence in one's straits is missed.[23]

We have seen that mundane fears should be transposed into fear of heaven. This latter may be understood in two ways: fear of punishment and a fear which results in a sense of God's exaltedness.[24] The former is a self-centered one, the latter, a gift of God. The goal is attainment of the latter, though the former must be experienced—in order to be fought.[25] R. Mendel's understanding of the two modes of the "fear of heaven" may be brought into sharper relief if viewed in light of Maharal's discussion of this theme in *Netiv Ahavat ha-Shem*.[26]

Maharal's immediate concern is to distinguish between fear and love of God. The difference lies in the different existential predisposition the individual brings to the encounter. Love of God resides in a "good" heart, stripped of perceptions generated by "sinister" impulses. The fearer of God, however, brings his own fears and anxieties to the religious experience:

כאשר נכנס בעל היראה לפני המלך נראה אליו כמדת
היראה **כפי מה שהוא עם השי׳ת**, ודבר זה הוא קצף המלך
כי כל יראה הוא מדת קצף, ולפיכך נזדעזע מפני קצפו של
מלך...ואמר כאשר נכנס בעל היראה נגלה אליו **כפי מדתו**
ולכך נגלה אליו בקצף ולא שהיה קצף על בעל היראה כי זה
לא שייך, רק כי כך **נגלה אליו כפי מדתו ביראה**

God appears frightening to a person simply because one's own fears are projected onto Him. God is revealed according to the beholder's own quality and, if that be anxiety, God will appear to be angry. This account is an important extension of what Maharal says about the different religious orientations one may opt for.[27] If one is oriented by the natural order, God will relate "naturally," and He will be perceived "naturally" (i.e., in anger). If, however, one is oriented by a transcendent order, struggling to resist the pull of perceived reality (i.e., frightful reality), God is revealed from that perspective. God as He is[28] is not angry; it is the fearer's anxious perception which makes Him so.

R. Mendel assumes Maharal's understanding of the distinction between the two modes of "fear." Fear of God's punishment does not have exalted religious significance because it cannot transcend one's self-centered perceptions.[29] A sense of God's "anger" merely reflects one's personal anxieties, which must not be projected onto the divine. "My fear" and "my anger" must be fought in order to attain what in *devekut* is perceived as God's "kiss."[30]

This "consolation" leads into R. Mendel's higher mode of "fear," the one which results in a sense of being raised by God' exaltedness, *yir'at ha-rom'mut*.[31] This "fear" is identified with divine grace, because the "fearer" who is in a sense "dead," senses being raised and infused with divine "life." Having experienced a trial, a situation which renders one *mah*, one clings to God's supportiveness and feels energized. The elevation which is occurring is that of the "dead" being quickened to "life." One is raised to being, from a situation of "what am I."[32]

The phrase *yir'at ha-rom'mut* does not appear in ethical literature before Hasidism, and the meaning attached to the phrase in R. Mendel's writing reflects Maharal's influence. Two passages in Maharal's writing may be integrated to produce this sense and to suggest the coinage of

yir'at ha-rom'mut. In *Netiv ha-Yir'ah*, Maharal
identifies *yir'ah* with being "as if one is not."[33]
In the Sermon for Shabbat ha-Gadol, in a passage already examined, the following appears:[34]

האדם הזה מצד עצמו הוא מה אבל מצד שהשית׳ **מגביה**
שפלים...האדם הוא מאד...מצד השית׳ אשר לו כח...
ורוממות...

It is God's exaltedness which elevates one who
is "as if he is not" to a state of great power.

For R. Mendel, the term "fear," of the psychological, self-centered kind, refers not only to
the state of being frightened. It connotes as well
a whole range of emotions, including shame,
regret, anger, grief, a desire to "cover up" a
fault[35]—impulses which arise from failure and
are characterized generically as "foreign
fears."[36] R. Mendel does not allow these to be
ignored or repressed;[37] they must simply not be
indulged, and any desire[38] to dwell on feelings
which alienate one from *devekut* must be
fought. R. Mendel considers the melancholia
which follows failure, even religious failure, as
rooted in pride.[39] It does not suit one to fail; that
is the source of profound regret which results in
mental depression. It is not a religious impulse,
but rather a self-serving one.[40] If one failed
religiously, therefore, the "false construction
which the mind is prone to create should be torn
down,"[41] and one's burden should be lightened.
A struggle should be waged to give one's "self"

Bezalel Safran

up, i.e., the self-inflicted mental state which purports to be the real self.[42] Being in *devekut*, the true "self," the real "face," is God. By indulging self-centered "fears," one is "having other gods in God's face"[43] and thwarting the divine presence within from taking charge.[44]

In fact, depression is not simply a barrier to divine service, it is almost idolatry[45] because one thereby demonstrates resentment of God's will. Being in *devekut*, one would view even lapses, one's *ayin*, as a divine message and be reconciled to dependence on the divine, not attempt to deny the dependence, which the lapse demonstrates, by feelings of guilt.[46]

The term *ayin* is therefore used in several related senses. On the one hand, *ayin* is a sense of failure and shame.[47] On the other hand, it means a leap to the divine and exclusive preoccupation with Him, nothing else *(ayin)* but Him, with no extraneous thoughts to distract.[48] Furthermore, with the very onset of a potentially fearsome provocation, before letting one's self be impressed by the unfavorable mundane implications, one should seek to be *ayin*, beyond the oppressive pressures of the temporal. In that realm, no "breakage" can occur. In this passage, the meaning of *ayin* shifts imperceptibly: an exclusive preoccupation with the divine becomes a realm where the divine predominates and bars harm to those in *devekut*: one is "a temple in the divine camp."[49] A focus for all these convergent meanings is pro-

vided by a comment of the Baal Shem Tov, cited
by R. Mendel in the course of discussing the
"poor ones" (מדריגת דלים). Aware as "poor
ones" are of their many "deaths," as it were,
chastened by their failures and lapses, they
know that, whatever their achievements, they
could not possibly be their own. Stubbornly
clinging to the divine, they are not "broken" by
their inadequacy. What keeps them intact and
persevering is divine will—not merit but *ayin*,
now in the sense of God's gracious will.[50]

We have seen that *ayin* is the conversion of
self-centered fear into a fear of heaven, i.e.,
devekut. If allowed to fester in one's consciousness, however, without being immediately
checked, "fears" will weigh down on the divine
presence within and frustrate its power. But
devekut is threatened by another force as well,
the barrier created by the self-satisfaction that
comes with religious achievement. R. Mendel,
like Maharal, views these two tendencies as diversions from left and right respectively.[51] R.
Mendel, too, knows them as "extremes" or
opposites,[52] but primarily as פניות,[53] i.e., digressions from *devekut*.

R. Mendel cautions the worshiper against the
pitfalls of depression as well as of self-
gratification.[54] He cites the Baal Shem Tov's
view[55] that both of these diversions are rooted
in pride, i.e., it suits one to excel religiously just

as it is unbecoming to fail. But divine service "must be for the sake of the Shekinah only, not even a modicum may be self-serving," so both aberrations must be resisted. Pleasing stimuli or disconcerning irritants, therefore,[56] are not received at face value, preoccupied as one is with relating these immediately to the experience of *devekut*.[57] To savor satisfaction for the achievement, to take pleasure even in religious work, is to vitiate the purity of the divine service, which must be offered for the sake of heaven exclusively.[58] Furthermore, one may not share credit for religious achievement with the divine, for in *devekut* one knows that it is He who achieves.[59] In *devekut*, being *ayin*, one is a musical instrument played by the divine. Can an instrument take pride in the pleasing tones being produced through it?[60] Can the person who is "nothing" take pride in successful moral achievement? The self is "nothing" in the sense that it (the self) is a result of forces right and left obstructing *devekut*. These aberrations are there to spur a connection with the order of *devekut*, through their arrest;[61] it is in this way that their "elevation" is achieved.

To take pride for religious achievement, as we have seen, is to arrogate God's achievment for one's self. The Baal Shem Tov, in an aforementioned passage,[62] carries this one step further in comparing one's worship with another's. To consider one's own religious service to be superior to another's is objectionable on grounds analogous to those just mentioned. One's fellow person was simply not so well endowed by the divine. In fact, "if God had not given one His *devekut*, one would do no better than the lowliest creature." R. Mendel cites this statement in *Likutei Amarim* as the Besht's,[63] and proceeds to base one of his sermons in *P'ri Etz* on it.[64] And what began as an admonition to humility becomes what R. Mendel views as a cornerstone of true faith.

One cannot judge anyone else's shortcomings; it is divine causes—often inscrutable——which have given one person certain advantages that another lacks. Encounter with a person who is religiously or morally lacking, therefore, rather than arousing criticism and censure, kindles one's own sense of vulnerability and dependence on divine love. Acutely aware as the "poor" one is of his own profound inadequacy, and, grateful for the unconditional divine support extended notwithstanding it, he is moved to "love all of Israel." He knows how much like everyone else he is: without the benefit of God's lovingkindness, he would be just like the "sinner."[65]

This sense is depicted by R. Mendel as התלהבות— another term newly coined by early Hasidism—and it entails a dual awareness. On the one hand is a trenchant, chastening self-criticism culminating in a self-knowing realization of how undeserving one is of divine generosity.[66] On the other hand, this very realization heightens love and joy in the divine, who enlivens one through His grace.[67] Moved by divine love and joy filling up "a void in the heart of the true lover of God"—a void, because "on his own he has nothing"—he turns to other people, including sinners, with empathy and love, in the knowledge of their common vulnerability, and in humility, recognizing his own religious success is due to divine grace.

ובאהבה זו ממילא יתקשר לכל באי עולם ובני אדם כיוצא בו אחרי היות האהבה שפע ברכה עליונה...כי לא זכה מנפשו אליו, וא'א כלל לעשותה ולזכות בה, אבל ברצונה הקבה' נתנה לו, ואם היה נותן מתנה זו לחברו היה חברו כיוצא בו מתלהב לשמו ית', וא'כ במה נחשב הוא מחברו?

Such a far-reaching identification with other people's shortcomings is the preparation for the next threshold. Every experience, even one which entails opposition or provocation by other people, is lived as if it is orchestrated by God, as rooted in His Will.[69] Faults perceived in others are reflections of one's own vulnerability and a signal for contact with the divine which enables one to overcome these faults, latent or overt.[70] The "fear" or resentment of others should be immediately converted to fear of heaven. It is the "voice of God" one hears in criticism or opposition by others, and resenting or judging them is tantamount to judging God.[71]

The leitmotif for R. Mendel is a Talmudic passage in *Berakhot* 20a, cited at the beginning and end of the sermon and echoed in fragments throughout. The passage is concerned with an apparent spiritual decline: "How is it that for the former generations miracles were performed and for us miracles are not performed?" The former generations are epitomized by the years when concern was focused on the Mishnaic order of Nezikin and during which, when R. Judah used to remove one shoe, rain would come. In later years, though study is more extensive and ramified, "we torment ourselves and cry loudly, and no notice is taken of us." The answer given is that "the former generation used to be ready to sacrifice their lives for the sanctity of God's name, while we do not."

Casting his discussion in context of this passage provides R. Mendel with a literary frame, enabling him to explicate some themes, imply others.

The concern with Nezikin, the section of the Mishnah dealing with torts and damages, is interpreted generically. In former years, special care was exercised in regard to personal relations. This special care is linked to Hillel's view that "what is hateful to you, do not do to your colleague" is the quintessence of divine service. More concretely stated, since all is from God, provocation by another ("what is hateful to you") needs to be transferred to another dimension, the order of *devekut*.[72] Indeed, R. Mendel seems to suggest that the reference to Rab Judah's removing his shoe is linked with the removing of the shoe in Ruth 4:7 which is the Biblical basis for laws of transfer of possession through a swap. [73] In former years, a "fear" of being accosted by one or a temptation to judge a fault in another was "swapped" mentally for a call from the Source: challenge to fear God, to judge one's self.[74] Maharal, too, employs the term "swapping" in the sense of *devekut*: a transfer of mundane desires or frustrations to a transcendent "second world."[75]

Such *devekut* in the days of R Judah resulted in "rain," an effluence of God's love. Relating self-centered fear to its source in the divine would generate divine "life."[76] Rounding out his instruction, R. Mendel supplies some "cues" on how to relate fear or resentment to their "roots" in the supernal realm ultimately energized by God's love. If mundane fear is experienced as "God's honor," as relatedness to God's power, it then becomes a source of soothing love.[77]

It follows that the capacity of former generations to sacrifice, to give themselves over completely for the sake of God's name, expresses itself in a suppression of the self's urge to perceive a provocative social situation as a mundane event.[78] Other people are "names of God"[79] and self-judgment,[80] occasioned by witnessing others' faults,[81] is a vehicle for conceding one's own vulnerability and dependence on divine aid to overcome one's own faults.

Such a gesture of stripping an event of its "natural veneer"[82] enables one to relate the seven "base emotions" to their root. The seven lower Kabbalistic *sephirot* are essentially the totality of human emotional possibilities (e.g., love, fear or resentment, admission of failure) which are related to their root in the divine.[83] Elevating these human urges, i.e., arresting them for the sake of the divine, expands the boundaries of the sacred realm. In such an atmosphere, when the divine reality is unified through suppression of "right and left" impulses, even mundane reality is enhanced.[84] In other words, when only the divine dimension is acknowledged to be real,[85] not "natural" perceptions of self, "rain," the divine love, sustains even the temporal realm.

Related to this discussion is the meaning of the "love which does not depend on a mundane thing." Both Maharal and R. Mendel intepret the well-known text in *Avot* 5:18-19 as alluding to the discrepancy between this kind of love and a "controversy not for the sake of heaven." The relationship between "controversy which *is* for the sake of heaven" and the "love which is *not* dependent on a mundane thing" is interpreted homiletically. The two are viewed as cause and effect, respectively, of struggle for unity and its achievement. Because it presupposes suppression of "right" and "left" impulses, the love is identified with the unified reality of *devekut*. A self-centered perception, oriented by the "evil urge," creates controversy not for the sake of heaven, i.e., it contravenes the ideal of *devekut* and generates duality; it makes reality appear fragmented and threatening.

But this apparent "fragmentation" (controversy) is a spur to struggle for self-transcendence, an opportunity to relate "fire" or "water," fear or love to their source as "words of the living God."[86] Were it not for the need to struggle constantly "for the sake of heaven", *devekut* would be static, and the blissful sense of God's providing life continuously would be absent. That is why God sustains fragmentation[87] and, furthermore, energizes what would be a vain effort if one attempted to leap to transcendence by one's own resources.[88]

The ideal of sacrificing one's self for the divine is discussed by R. Mendel, not only in connection with an achieved *devekut*, but also—and particularly so—with a failed effort. A lapse one "falls" into is a valuable experience. It enables one to "return one's energies" to the Creator;[89] in other words, to acknowledge that one cannot endure without divine aid.[90]

ולהיות האדם המצטדק הרבה ועוסק בתורה...בלא
התלהבות ושום דביקות והצליח, שלא בא לידי נסיון שום
דבר, להבין פחיתותו שאינו יכול לעמוד בנסיון וכל כחותיו
קשורים בגשמים, ומוכן ומזומן לעבור על כל דבר רע בהגיע
לידו **מלבד שהנסיונות לא הגיעו לידו**, ולכן **לפעמים מזדמן
לו מעשה רשע**, בכדי שיתן לבו להבין שאינו שלם עם ד'
ויתלהב לתשובה להשיב את כל כחותיו ותענגיו אל ד'

Once again, we encounter the term *hitlahavut* in the sense of "purging" one's self. The word is employed here in the sense of being spurred to

conceding, as a result of failures, that one cannot withstand the trial when it comes. As long
as one is not reconciled with being exposed and
dependent, one is not "whole (reconciled) with
God."[91] This "wholeness" *(shlemut)* enables
one to "return one's energies to the divine," i.e.,
to admit one's dependence.[92] The divine aid on
which one depends is extended in the guise of
"causes." Control of anger or fear may be successful because of the embarrassment generated
by being uncontrolled; if the "cause" of shame
is not present, there is no assurance of virtue.[94]

David's fall was a result of his sense that he
"achieved" superior virtue and was no longer a
mere function of divine "causes." Following his
fall, he became reconciled to his dependence
and acknowledged his perpetual need for divine
aid. As spiritual leader of his people, his fall and
the "return"[95] of energies to the divine was
paradigmatic[96]—and a means through which he
might identify with his fellow people's
vulnerabilities:[97]

וכן דוד המלך עליו השלום מגודל צדקותיו ובטחונו בעצמו
שכבר החזיר את כל כחותיו לדבקו בו יתברך אמר (תהלים
כו:ב) בחנני ד' ונסני, ואף על פי שאמר לו הנסיון שינסהו
אעפכ' אחרי הסרת שמירת ית' מאתו נכשל בכדי להבינו
שאין שום אפשרות הבטחון בעצמו בעודו בגוף...וכמאמר
אלמלא הק'בה עוזרו אינו יכול לו. וזהו ע'ז ד: לא היה דוד
ראוי לאותו מעשה אלא כדי להורות תשובה —

Our discussion of R. Mendel began with the
observation that there is close resemblance

between Maharal's notion of *devekut* and R. Mendel's. The parallels are striking because common themes are often expressed in identical terms. The terminological bond between the two writers unites their treatments of mystical experience.

Maharal's newly-coined mystical vocabulary, his special use of *ayin* as well as its correlation with a mystical realm "beyond time"[98] are both employed by R. Mendel. Analogously, the special sense in which fear and love are understood by Maharal is adopted in R. Mendel's writing. The transfer of experiences from the mundane to a realm of *devekut*—a theme common to both—is frequently evoked in common modes. These relationships as well as the other thematic resemblances cited in this article demonstrate a knowledge of Maharal by R. Mendel and an affinity toward his understanding of traditional texts. Maharal himself did not perceive his literary production as the creation of a system. In fact, in the introduction to *Netivot Olam* he emphasizes his concern with an interpretation of Rabbinic statements and their collation—nothing else.[99]

But Maharal's ideas do lend themselves to systematization. The Hasidic temper found them congenial, explicated them, cast them into a system and popularized them for large groups of people. That R. Mendel did not consider Maharal's works accessible to everyone but worthy of popularization may be inferred from their omission from his list of recommended ethical literature,[100] though he cites *Derek Hayim* in his own work. Maharal's writing spoke to R. Mendel's own religious experience and his understanding of the Baal Shem Tov. When he went public, Maharal's work provided a convenient literary and conceptual frame.

Preface

[1]On the perception of Maharal in nineteenth-century Hasidism, see "Mavo," *Perushei Maharal mi-Prague*, ed. M. S. Kasher (Jerusalem, 1958), pp. 27-32. On the required reading of Maharal's works, see pp. 27, 28.

[2]G. Scholem, *Major Trends in Jewish Mysticism* (New York, 1978), p. 339.

[3]A Gottesdiener, *Ha-Maharal mi-Prague* (Jerusalem, 1976), p. 54.

[4]B. Sherwin, *Mystical Theology and Social Dissent: The Life and Works of Judah Loew of Prague* (New Jersey, 1982), pp. 52-54, 130-131, 138-140, 164-165. See also additional bibliography in the notes.

[5]On R. Mendel's *aliyah* to Tiberias in 1777 and continued correspondence with the Hasidim in Belorussia; see J. Barnai, ed., *'Iggerot Hasidim me'Eretz Yisrael* (Jerusalem, 1980). The volume contains all the extant correspondence. The theoretical teaching is contained in three volumes, *Peri ha-'Aretz, Peri 'Etz* and *Likutei Amarim.*

Amarim, which tends to definition and essayistic formulations more so than the other two. Once R. Mendel's thought structures are clear and distinct, they may serve as a basis for understanding the homilies of *Peri 'Etz* and *Peri ha-'Aretz*, works which deepen the premises of *Likutei Amarim*. To illustrate this relation, a seminal homily from *Peri 'Etz* has been selected and explicated. These three volumes are reprinted as *Sifrei Avot ha-Hasidut be'Eretz ha-Kodesh* (Jerusalem, 1969), and page references are to these editions.

The Jerusalem 1974 edition of *Peri ha-'Aretz* has integrated the homilies of *Peri ha-'Aretz* and *Peri 'Etz*, with some departures from the text of the above-mentioned editions. Rather, we have chosen to follow the text of *Peri 'Etz* (Zhitomir, 1874) because of the following statement on the title page, which testifies to the faithful reproduction of the text:

ספר פרי עץ מכבוד אדמו'ר גאון תפארת ישראל בוצינא קדישא עמודא
דנהורא אור המאיר לארץ כבוד שם קדושתו מוהר'ר מנחם מענדיל
מוויטיפסק זצוקל'לה בעה'מח ספר פרי הארץ אשר מקום ישיבתו היה.
באה'ק טבריא תוב'ב והעתק אות באות מכתב יד הנמצא תחת יד הרב
הקדוש ונורא אדמו'ר וכו' מהו'ר אהרן מטשורנאבל זצוקללההה אשר
היה מנחה שלוחה לו מעה'ק ירושלים.

Professor Twersky suggested that the special care in copying (העתק אות באות) is testimony to the reverence in which R. Mendel was held by R. Aaron of Chernobyl.

[6]"Mavo," p. 29, n.7, for this reference and expression of similar attitudes by R. Abraham of Sochatzow and others.

[7]Maharal is conscious of writing in fragments, which he expects the reader to collate. He terms this method writing בפרקים. Such reference is not to *Derek Hayim*, his commentary on פרקי אבות, because this work is referred to by name (see, e.g., *Gevurot ha-Shem* [New York, 1969], p. 311). Conversely, a theme may be noted בפרקים and not be found in *Derek Hayim* at all (e.g., *Nezah Yisrael* [New York, 1969], p. 92). The term, then, is employed to suggest that a given theme is treated in different contexts, and that to get a full view one needs to collate all the "chapters." In *Derek Hayim*, such a theme is, e.g., צלם

אלקים concerning which there are at least ten "פרקים"
scattered throughout the work. Concerning repetition,
Maharal explains some of it as an attempt to cast a theme
from different perspectives (*Derek Hayim*, p. 266:
ופירשנו הדבר בבחינות שונות זה מזה כדי להעמיד אותך על נכול)

Part I

[1]*Derek Hayim* Introduction.

[2]The edition used in the preparation of this article is H.
Pardes, ed. (Tel Aviv, 1980). Other references to Mahar-
al's works are to the series *Kol Kitvei Maharal mi-Prague*
(New York, 1969).

[3]These terms are used in apposition to each other
numerous times throughout Maharal's works. Units
which contain all of them interchangeably are *Netivot
Olam* II, *Netiv ha-Ka'as* and *Derek Hayim*, pp. 265-266:
מצוע, שווי and ישר. On the genesis of some of these terms,
see nn. 69, 84, 111.

[4]*Derek Hayim*, comment on *Avot* 2:14, p. 265:
וכן שנאת חנם ־ כי הבריות הם האדם ־ ואם שונא את האדם במה
שהוא אדם יש בו פחיתות וחסרון מצד שהוא אדם, כי אם הוא אדם
שלם לא יהיה שונא את הבריות אשר הם אדם רק שיש בו פחיתות במה
שהוא אדם, ולפיכך דבר זה מוציא את האדם מן העולם.

[5]It is clear from the context of the passage (n.4) that the
phrase רק שיש בו פחיתות במה שהוא אדם is not merely a
contrast to שהוא אדם שלם. Such contrast is achieved by the
first mention of the phrase: יש בו פחיתות וחסרון מצד שהוא
אדם. The repetition therefore is intended to indicate the
orientation of אדם שלם: other people's faults are not to be
resented but are a challenge to be reconciled to one's
faults, to being a lacking person.

[6]*Gevurot ha-Shem*, pp. 296-297; for the relationship
between הודאה and השלמה אל ד', see n.133.

[7]*Derek Hayim*, p. 266:
שנאת הבריות מוציא את האדם מן העולם מפני שהוא מתנגד אל
עצמו, שהרי **הבריות הם האדם עצמו** אשר ברא השי'ת בעולם...ובזה
[שנאת הבריות] נוטה אל ההעדר הגמור...וכן אם הבריות שונאים
אותו...

[8]Ibid., שנאת הבריות היא יציאה מן האדם עצמו שהוא היושר

[9]*Hidushei Aggadot* III *(Sanhedrin), p. 137:*

קשוט עצמך ואחר כך קשוט אחרים. פי' שהאדם קרוב לעצמו ממה שהוא לאחרים. ואם רוצה לדון את אחר קרוב לעצמו **לעשות דין בעצמו** ואם יעשה דין באחר ואין **עושה דין בעצמו** אין זה דיין כלל כי הדין בעצמו יותר קרוב והאדם עצמו קרוב.

Since judgment of others is really judgment of self, critical self-appraisal should precede an evaluation of one's fellow. Along these lines, see *Derek Hayim*, comment on *Avot* 2:4, p. 207:

אל תדון את חברך עד שתגיע למקומו, כלומר כי יש סבות הרבה לאדם ואם היתה אותה סבה בעצמה מתחדשת עליו כמו שהיא באה על חבירו היה עושה ג'כ מה שעושה חבירו...ולכן **אין לו לדון על עצמו.**

See also *Netivot Olam* II, *Netiv ha-Sh'tikah*, ch. 1, p. 100, for an interpretation of the Talmudic statement *(Kiddushin* 71b), כל הפוסל במומו פוסל:

האדם כמו עץ השדה והדבור הוא פרי שלו...וכמו שאין פרי רע יוצא מן שורש טוב ואין פרי טוב יוצא משורש רע, כך הדבור באדם כאשר מריב עם חבירו ופוגם אותו מורה זה על השורש שהפגם בא ממנו הוא רע, ולכן במומו דוקא פוסל, מפני כי הדבר הרע שיוצא ממנו הוא נמצא בו וכאשר גזע האילן הוא פגום כן יצא ממנו.

[10]*Tif'eret Yisrael*, ch. 7, p. 127.

ולהורות **כי מצות לא תעשה** נותנים לאדם סדר שלא יצא מן הראוי נתן לאדם מיד ז' מצות כולם מצות לא תעשה כמו שבארנו ענין אלו שבע מצות בחבור גבורת ד' ע'ש

The reference is to *Gevurot ha-Shem*, ch. 66, the source for the passage at the beginning of note 11.

[11]*Gevurot ha-Shem*, ch. 66, p. 307.

דינין - החטא הוא בנפשו שהוא מעוות משפט אמת והיושר אשר הוא בנפש האדם כי האמת והיושר בנפשו הוא, וזהו חטא הנפש כי אין יושר ומשפט רק בנפש השכלית.

This is the passage to which Maharal referred in the previous note. In this *Gevurot ha-Shem* passage, too, reference is made to the aforementioned text (n.10) in *Tif'eret Yisrael:*

נתן להם...ז' מצות שהם חבור העלה בעלול על ידי גזרותיו ומצוותיו, במה שהעלול מקבל גזירת ומצות העלה, ועוד יתבאר בספר תפארת ישראל.

Each of the passages contains essential elements concerning the nature of דינין and for a coherent understanding, they must be collated. This is an example of Maharal's writing ובפרקים, in fragments; and in this case he himself does the cross-referencing.

The cited passage from *Gevurot ha-Shem* should be read in light of two considerations, one substantive, one literary. a) דינין is viewed by Maharal as לא תעשה. b) In discussion of the previous three Noahide laws and subsequent three (דינין is in the middle) *the subject is the receiver* of these laws, e.g.,

עז׳-כל החטאים אא׳ שיחטא בנפשו בלבד חוץ מעז׳ וג׳ע-הוא לבשר
מחמת יצרו שבגוף

This must be true of דינין as well. Hence the phrase - דינין
החטא הוא בנפשו means that the injustice one beholds is a reflection of one's own:

שהוא מעוות משפט אמת והיושר אשר הוא בנפש האדם

[12]*Netivot Olam* I, *Netiv ha-Din*, ch. 1. The first chapter of *Netiv ha-Din* is introduced by the statement המשפט הוא
היושר בעצמו. And, indeed, the chapter in its entirety is most intelligible when דין and משפט are understood as acceptance of God's judgment. This meaning of דין is suggested in the comment on *Avot* 1:16,

העולם קיים על הדין והאמת והשלום...בעולם התחתון[של דין] **מקבל**
הדין מן המושלים...שכל ענין עולם התחתון הכל גזירת דין

and reinforced in *Netiv ha-Din* ch. 1—

ולפיכך נתן המשפט אל ישראל...כי השית׳ הוא העלה והעלה יש לו
עלול, וישראל יש עליהם **משפט** העלול מן השית׳...ולפיכך המשפט
הוא שייך אל ישראל...ועל ידי המשפט הקב׳ה מתעלה בעולמו...כי
השית׳ אשר אליו המשפט בפרט, כאשר המשפט הוא בעולם הזה, אז
מתגבה השופט על הנשפט. אבל אם השי׳ת בעצמו עושה משפט
בעולמו, ובעולם אין משפט אין מתגבה כ׳כ.

(see also comment on *Avot* 3:3, concerning קבלת גזירת
השית). The phrase ובעולם אין משפט refers to acceptance of God's justice which "He makes in the world." This meaning is confirmed by the immediate context, as well as by the larger one, which speaks of משפט as demonstrating

the state of עלול, of being acted upon by God—and acquiescing in it, an attitude through which God is exalted. The passage continues:

רק כאשר המשפט הוא בעולם הזה. ובזה ממליכין את המלך המשפט כאשר התחתונים עצמם רוצים במשפט, כאשר **עושים משפט, ובזה מקבלים עליהם מלך המשפט** ומגביהים אותו.

The phrase עושים משפט is to be conjoined with מקבלים עליהם מלך המשפט, and also with n.9, עושה דין בעצמו.

כי אין יושר ומשפט רק **בנפש השכלית**[13], end of passage at beginning of n.11.

[14]The second introduction to *Gevurot ha-Shem* constitutes Maharal's introduction to miracles: p. 7—

העולם התחתון הוא **עולם הטבע** יש לו התדבקות **בעולם הנבדל** — ומשם הנסים באים...כמו שיש לעולם הטבע סדר מסודר נוהג על פי טבעו כך יש לנסים סדר גם כן, כי הנסים בעולם במה שיש לעולם קשור וחבור והתאחדות עם העולם הנבדל...כשם שראוי לעולם להיות נוהג על פי טבעו והנהגתו, כך ראוי לישראל במה שהם **דבקים** בעולם הנבדל שיהי׳ להם נסים מסודרים, הנה יש לנסים סדר מסודר מן השית׳, ואין דבר מן הנסים יקרא שנוי בנבראים כי אנו אומרים כי הכל בסדר מסודר מן השם יתברך.

p. 11

והדבר המסודר מאתו ית׳ מצד הבריאה, והמסודר מאתו ע׳י רחמים, שני דברים הם, זה מצד הסדור וזה מצד הרחמים, ולרחמים יש סדר מיוחד.

On p. 15, the order of דמיון is identified with חמר and גשם, and contrasted with the order of שכל which transcends them. And pp. 15-16

עמידת השמש ליהושע...הנה היתה השמש בשתי בחינות, כפי חלוף המדרגות תלך מצד הטבע ותעמוד בצד בלתי טבעי, כי כשם שראוי שתלך מצד הטבעי כך יש **בחינה שכלי׳** שבאמצע השמים יש לה עמידה כמו שהתבאר, והוא בחינה שכלית ואין זה טבעי, ולכך הי׳ לה עמידה במדריגה בלתי טבעית.

See also *Derek Hayim*, comment on *Avot* 3:6, p. 307: השכל מתעלה על העולם הגשמי. For a discussion of Maharal's theory of miracles—the simultaneity of natural and metaphysical dimensions of reality—in context of medieval Jewish thought, and for bibliography on previous treatments, see T. Ross, "Ha-Nes ke-Meimad Nosaf ba-Hagut ha-Maharal mi-Prague," *Da'at* XVII (Summer 1986) 81-96.

[15]Ibid., p. 17

כי הבלתי טבעי אינו תמידי. אך הוא לפי שעה ומאחר שהוא לפי שעה אפשר   שהוא ג׳כ לנמצא זה שהוא צריך לאותו דבר ויש לו **הכנה** לזה — ונמצא לו דרך נס בלתי טבעי ולא לשאר הנמצאים.

On the correlation between acting "unnaturally" in a mode which is נבדל and sharing in a supernatural (נבדל) reality, see the comment on *Avot* 5:3 concerning Abraham's trials: (p. 528)

שיש בעולם מדריגה עליונה **נבדלת** אשר מורה על זה מספר עשרה, כך נתנסה אברהם בי׳ נסיונות דוקא, כי על ידי אלו עשרה נסיונות נעשה אברהם ג׳כ **נבדל** מן הטבע לגמרי שזהו ענין הנסיון כמו שהתבאר. (p. 527)

כי אם אין המנוסה נוהג שלא בטבע, אינו יכול לעמוד בנסיון

[16]*Netivot 'Olam* II, *Netiv ha-Ka'as,* ch. 1, p. 236, see characterization of Bet Hillel in contrast to שאר בני אדם.

[17]Further development of the themes discussed in this paragraph is provided in *Netivot 'Olam* I, *Netiv ha-'Avodah*, ch. 1. ישר is linked with a)אחדות, a panentheistic view of reality, and hence with b) relating natural impulses to a divine order. The term employed for "relating" is תולה or נתלה. See n.108 on Maharal's usage of this term and for elaboration of its meaning. On complementary usage of **אחדות** see notes 26, 113; part II, n.78.

On "נפש" in the phrase "נפש שכלית," used in the passage covered by n.11, see n.78.

[18]*Gevurot ha-Shem*, ch. 67, p. 309:

שהוא ית׳ כמו שהוא גדול על הכל, כן יתברך כולל הכל.

and more elaborately, p. 181:

[האמונה] האחת שהוא משגיח בתחתונים...[האמונה] השנית שהכל הוא ביד ד׳, ואין דבר חוץ ממנו וזהו אמונת מציאות השי׳ת, כי בודאי הכל מודים במציאות השי׳ת, רק **שלא יאמר שאינו הכל** חס ושלום ויוכל לצאת מרשותו, לכך אמונת מציאות השית׳ **שהוא הכל ואין דבר חוץ ממנו יתברך.**

[19]מוסר כולל. The phrase is employed in relation to *Avot* 2:1, 3:1 and 4:1. What makes these particular teachings מוסר כולל is that human fears and loves are related to the divine in the special mode that Maharal will set forth. Much of the discussion in this article revolves round this theme. The peculiarly "כולל" aspect of the above-mentioned *mishnayot* is discussed at the very end of the comments on *Avot* 2:1 and 3:1, and the theme of מסתפק" "בעצמו in *Avot* 4:1.

[20]In *Derek Hayim* the main discussion is the comment on *Avot* 3:16, but with important correlatives on *Avot* 2:1, end, 3:1, end, and 5:22, end. See also *Gevurot ha-Shem*, ch. 67.

[21]This first sense of צלם א' is elaborated in *Derek Hayim*, comment on *Avot* 3:16, pp. 346-349:

לא...שהאדם הוא בצלם דמותו יתברך אבל על הבריאה נאמר
והבריאה היא בעולם הגשמי, אשר בעולם הגשמי יש שם דמות וצלם.

[22]Ibid., p. 353; comment on *Avot* 2:14, p. 263 and references mentioned in n.377 (p. 263); also (p. 264), concerning restraint of anger to avoid loss of עולם הבא. For just how seriously the provocative encounter is treated, see *Netivot Olam* II, *Netiv ha-'Anavah*, ch. 8, p. 19.

[23]See *Hidushei Aggadot* II (on *Gittin*), p. 93.

[24]*Netivot Olam* II, *Netiv ha-Bitahon*, p. 235.

[25]Ibid.,

ואין אל מה שאמר השכם והערב עליהן לבית המדרש רמז בכתוב, רק
שהכתוב אומר שידום לד' לצפות ולקוות אל השית' כי הוא ילחום
מלחמתו- ודבר זה אינו רק כשהוא בוטח בו יתברך, א'כ הוא מוסר עצמו
אל השם ית' וגם הוא משכים ומעריב לבית המדרש ובזה הוא חלקו של
הקב'ה לגמרי...כי הבטחון הוא **על השכל** וההשכמה לביהמ'ד ללמוד
תורה גב' אל השכל ואז מלחמתו מלחמת השם.

"God's war" (מלחמת השם) is used in two senses in this passage. It is God's war because through his (דום לד') דומיה God fights his battles:

ופי' דום כלומר שהוא ישתוק ולא יעשה דבר והשית' יעשה מלחמתו
But it is also Mar Ukba's war for the sake of God: ואז

מלחמתו מלחמת ד'. Through his struggle (מלחמתו) to muster
trust, he gives himself over to God, (מוסר עצמו אל השם ית'),
and gravitates to the realm beyond reason, כי הבטחון הוא
על השכל. Maharal's unique usage of the term מלחמות השם
is probably determined by the Talmudic interpretation
(*Kiddushin* 30b) of the latter part of Numbers 21:14 which
creates a new perspective for the beginning of the verse:
על כן יאמר בספר מלחמות השם.

שכל is used by Maharal both in the sense of שכל אנושי
(as here) as well as שכל אלקי נבדל. Context—or his explanation—helps determine which is the relevant meaning.
For Maharal's distinction between the two senses, see, for
example, *Nezah Yisrael*, ch. 31, p. 144. The "engagement
with Torah" mentioned here is to be understood in light
of Maharal's usages in *Derek Hayim*. In comment on *Avot*
3:6, עסק בתורה is valued because:

עוסק בתורה מתעלה על העולם הגשמי כי השכל מתעלה על העולם
הגשמי

or comment on *Avot* 1:12, p. 152, concerning עמל בתורה,
understood as מגביר השכל על החמר.

[26]*Hidushei Aggadot (Bava Mezia)* III, p. 45:

ענין נגעים הם מקרים מתהוים בעולם, והם פגעי הזמן, כמש' (תהלים
צא'), לא תאונה אליך רעה ונגע לא יקרב באהליך, ושם מזכיר ענין פגעי
הזמן ומקריו, וכמו שקראו ר'זל המזמור הזה שיר של פגעים...והשי'
השגחתו פשוטה משיג המציאות משולל ומסולק מן המקרה, ולכך כל
ספק מקרה הוא טהור, בשביל כי השגה הפשוטה **נבדלת** מן המקרה עד
שאין מציאות אל המקרה, כאשר אין מוכרח לתת מציאות אל המקר-
ה...שאר הנמצאים מצד שאין השגתם כל כך פשוטה להשיג מציאות
העולם בעצם מסולק מן המקרה, ואין השגתם **נבדל** מן המקרה ולכן
נותנין יותר מציאות אל פגעי הזמן והם מקריו...

ורבה שהיה מטהר הספק מורה על שהשגתו פשוטה. ובשביל השגה
הפשוטה שבו היה דבקותו בו ית', **ועל ידו היה דבקות ואחדות** לשאר
נמצאים, שמצד הנמצאים בעצמם היה ריחוק והבדל, ומצד רבה נמצא
האחדות, **והוא שלימות העולם**...ועל ידו קבלו אמיתות ההשגה.

God's unity is enhanced through Rabbah, since the duality of physical (or דמיון, as it is alluded to above, n.14) and
metaphysical is denied by him and reality is apprehended

as divine only. One in *devekut* emulates the divine in struggling to deny the reality of פגעי הזמן. In light of this passage, see *Netivot Olam* I, *Netiv ha-'Avodah*, ch. 4, end.

This conception of *devekut* to the divine implying transcendence of the "accidents" (מקרים) of the mundane is elaborated as well by Maimonides in his Guide III:51, also with references to Psalm 91; as well as by Naḥmanides' comments on Deut. 11:22, Leviticus 18:4, Job 36:7.

[27]See references in n.23.

[28]צלם א' in this second sense is elaborated in *Derek Hayim*, comment on *Avot* 3:16, pp. 349-355: ואם אתה רוצה לפרש מלת בצלמו, הצלם שיש לו להשית' לפי האמת...

[29]*Derek Hayim*, p. 264.
כי זה ארחות חיים לעולם הבא להביא את האדם מן עולם הזה שהוא עולם הגשמי אל עולם הנבדל הוא עולם הבא.

[30]Ibid., and *Hidushei Aggadot (Shabbat)* I, p. 80, col. 2, וענין הצלם הזה. Also suggested here, and explicated several times in *Derek Hayim*, is the notion of עולם הבא as עולם שני, into which one may "leap" in *devekut*. See, for example, comment on *Avot* 3:3: כי העולם יש כאן עולם שני עולם הבא, ולכן העולם נברא בבית. An oft-repeated exegesis on Isaiah 26:4, "בטחו בד' עדי עד כי בי־ה ד' צור עולמים" and the meaning assigned to it in *Menakot* 29b, אלו שני עולמות שברא הקב'ה אחד ביור ואחד בהא also emphasizes the simultaneity of the two orders—in this world. In a comment on *Avot* 5:1 *(Derek Hayim)*:
נרמז במה שכתוב. כי בי־ה ד' צור עולמים, העולם הזה נברא בהא והעולם הבא ביוד, מפני כי היוד מספר עשרה, שמספר עשרה שייך לכל דבר שיש לו מעלה קדושה, לכך השכינה עם מספר זה.
אבל עולם הזה נברא בהא כי ההא יש בה שני חלקים, לרמוז כי **העולם** הזה יש בו שני דברים. שהוא **עולם גשמי**, ומכל מקום **דבק בו** גם כן **מדריגה עליונה קדושה**, והההא היא ד' [הרומז זת לעולם הגשמי] ובתוך הד' יש בו יוד [שרומזת על עוהב]

[31]*Derek Hayim*, comment on *Avot* 3:16: p. 349:
הצלם...לא בא רק על עיקר הצלם והתמונה, שכל דבר שיש לו צלם ודמות יש לו זיו, והוא עיקר הצלם והדמות דהיינו האור והזיו של הצלם.

[32]Ibid., p. 350:

חזהו אמרם במס' בבא בתרא (נח.) נסתכלתי בשני **עקביו** של אדם הראשון, **עקביו** שהוא **סוף שפלות** שהרי הוא רחוק מן הפנים, שהוא עיקר הצלם הוא דומה לגלגל חמה שהוא הזוהר העליון, כי הניצוץ הזה שהי' מקבל אדם הראשון הוא ניצוץ עליון נבדל, ולכן עקביו דומים לגלגל חמה, ומפני כי יעקב אבינו הי' קרוב אצל אור הזה...

[33]Ibid. The previously cited paragraph ends with:

ועל זה אמר כי בצלם א' עשה את האדם כי אשר הוא **מקבל** הוא **נבדל** לגמרי, והבן הדברים האלו.

On מקבל as being reconciled see later, nn. 41, 42.

[34]*Nezah Yisrael,* introduction, p. 8:

שם **יעקב** נקרא מלשון שהי' יעקב מקטין עצמו כמו עקב ואין דבר יותר שפל מן העקב, ודבר זה הסבה שיהי' השית' מגביה אותו עד שיקרא ישראל על שם שרית עם אלקים ועם אנשים שכל המשפיל עצמו הקב'ה מגביה אותו.

[35]See the collection of sources on this theme in H. Pardes, *Perakim be-Mishnato shel ha-Maharal mi-Prague* (Tel Aviv, 1984), pp. 336-344.

[36]See for example *Derek Hayim*, the comment on *Avot* 5:8, *Gur Aryeh* on Genesis (B'nai Brak, 1972), pp. 153, 184.

[37]וזהו החולשה הוא אמת *Gur Aryeh*, p. 122.

[38]דבר והפכו. See the next note.

[39]*Derek Hayim*, comment on *Avot* 4:26. On שֵׁם מֵת p. 498. The discussion is based on p. 500, centering on דבר והפכו, in particular on the mode in which Maharal's questions 3 and 4 are answered (see n.616, ibid., p. 500).

Aside from the meaning of מֵת employed here, Maharal uses the term in two additional senses. See the passage covered by n.57 on the one hand, and the comment on *Avot* 6:4, on the other (ibid., pp. 675-676).

On מֵת as an ethical ideal in the latter sense, see Isaac Arama's exegesis of Ecclesiastes 4:2 (ושבח אני את המתים...מהחיים):

משבח אני אותם האנשים שנוטלים לעצמם לעצה הנכונה הצד...שאז'ל שאם ימות יחי' והם ימיתו עצמם בעולם הזה בהכריח תאותם והשקט המיית לבבם בכל חפציהם בהסתפק במועט המושג להם ע"ד טוב מעט

בצדקה (משלי טז'), זה כוון באומר **שכבר מתו, שכבר המיתו עצמה בחייהם**. וכמו שאמרו ז"ל (ברכות סג') אין דברי תורה מתקיימים אלא במי שממית עצמו עליה שנאמר (במדבר יט) אדם כי ימות באהל, מן החיים אשר הם חיים עדנה בעולם הזה בקצה האחרון כי הם אשר ימותו ע"ד האמת.

[40]*Netivot Olam* I, *Netiv 'Avodah*, ch. 4, end: ויורה על שם מקום, שהוא מקיים את אשר הוא מקום לו

[41]P. 151 *(Derek Hayim)*.

[42]*Netivot Olam* II, *Netiv ha-'Anavah*, end of chapter 2, p. 6; *Hidushei Aggadot (Sanhedrin)* III, pp. 184-185.

[43]*Derek Hayim*, comment on *Avot* 2:3 collated (as Maharal suggests) with comment on *Avot* 3:11, end:
...ודברים אלו ראוים להבין איך רוח המקום קשורה ברוח הבריות

[44]On this correlation see, for example, *Reshit Hokmah, Shaar ha-'Anavah*, ch. 3:
וכתב הר' יצחק דמן עכו ע"ה ששמע מפי ר"מ תלמידו של הר' יוסף גיקטיליא ע"ה כי האיש אשר ידבנו לבו לתקן מדותיו ולישר דרכיו ומעשיו ולרדוף אחרי הענוה בתכלית השלמות להיות עלוב ולא יעלוב שומע חרפתו ולא ישיב מיד תשרה עליו השכינה ולא יצטרך ללמוד מבשר ודם כי רוח אלקים תלמדנו עכ"ל

[45]"וְאֵין הָאָדם מקיים בו יתברך" in the passage covered by n.41.

[46]Ibid., ועצם החיות בעצמו הוא הקבלה שמקבל חיותו

[47]In context of the full passage covered by n.41, a reading of וְאֵין הָאָדם would be *non sequitur*. It should therefore be read וְאֵין הָאָדם. The term אַין would then be related to the cognate usages of אַיִן which occur in the notes that follow.

[48]G. Scholem, *Reshit ha-Kabbalah* (Jerusalem, 1948), p. 140.

[49]*Netivot Olam* II, *Netiv ha-Yir'ah*, ch. 1, p. 22.
אין היראה רק שעושה עצמו עלול והוא אצלו כאלו אינו כך הירא ד' עושה עצמו כְּאַיִן אצל עלתו...
See ibid., p. 21
היראה מה שמחשיב עצמו לְאַיִן וללא כלום לפני העלה יתברך
and also the passage in the next note.

50
היראה היא מגיע אל **עצם אלקותו יתברך** שהרי תרגום של אלקות הוא
דחלא שהוא לשון מורא, ומזה תראה כי **היראה** הוא **עצם האלקות**
ולפיכך אין דבר שהוא באוצרו רק היראה שהוא עם השית' לגמרי כמו...
שהאלקות הוא אצלו.

[51]The sustaining power is God's love, ibid., p. 22:
ועיקר היראה שהיא באה מכח האהבה As evoked in *Netiv*
ha-Ahavah, אהבה is identified with *devekut* (ibid., p. 44,
ובו תדבקון, זהו האהבה) and it is as much God's sustenance
of one as one's love for God: p. 38

כי השם ית' הוא **קיום האדם** ואא' זולתו ולפיכך **שייך אהבה אליו**, כי כל
דבר הוא אוהב דבר אשר הוא השלמתו **והוא ית' השלמת האדם**;
and p. 39

האהבה אל השית'...מה שאדם דבק בו ית' מוסר נפשו אליו, מתקשר בו
ומשלים אותו והיא האהבה האמתיח

again, p. 39

כי כל אהבה שיש בין האוהבים אף שהם דבקים זה בזה, מכל מקום יש
לכל אחד ואחד מציאות בעצמו, אבל האהבה אל השית' במה שהאדם
שב רוחו ונפשו אליו לגמרי עד שאין לאדם מציאות בעצמו ובזה הוא
מתדבק לגמרי בו...זהו האהבה הגמורה כאשר מוסר נפשו אל ד' כי בזה
דבק בו לגמרי והוא עצמו האהבה. ויתבאר לך כי יותר שייך אהבה אל
השית' במה שהאדם מוסר נפשו אל השית', ודבוק בו לגמרי והוא
אמיתת האהבה.

It follows that there is no love without fear, without the
sense of אַיִן ibid., p. 44.

[52]*Netivot Olam* II, *Netiv ha-Ka'as*, ch. 2, p. 239:
כי האדם הוא מסודר עם השי'ת שהוא עלה לו, וכאשר הוא כועס הוא
יוצא מן הסדר ולכן אמר...השכינה אינה חשובה כנגדו כי אינו מכיר
עלתו כאשר אינו יוצא מן הסדר.

[53]*Derek Hayim*, p. 266.
וכאשר יש כאן שנאת הבריות הוא מתנגד אל האדם עצמו על ידי שנאת
הבריות ובזה נוטה אל ההעדר הגמור...**ואיך אפשר שיהי' לו קיום בעולם**
כאשר הוא מתנגד אל עצמו והוא נוטה אל ההעדר?

[54]Ibid., האדם, who is the subject of *Derek Hayim*, is a
person in *devekut*. See Maharal's account, *Netiv ha-*
Yir'ah, ch. 6, end. p. 37, and beg. of n.97.

[55]See the previously cited passage in *Hidushei Aggadot (Shabbat)*, p. 80.

[56]Introduction to *Derek Hayim*, p. 65.

דרך ארץ נקרא דרך כי הוא **הדרך הישר** שאינו נוטה לימין ולשמאל רק הולך ביושר. כי כל דרך הולך **ביושר** נקרא **דרך חיים.**

[57]Ibid., p. 64. On the analogous usage of these terms connoting *devekut* see *Derek Hayim*, comment on *Avot* 5:17, p. 608, and, particularly, the comment on *Avot* 6:6, pp. 709-710:

ויש לך לדעת...כי הוא יתברך אחד ואין זולתו ולפיכך המציאות והחיים שיש לאדם ולכל הנמצאים, מפני שהוא יתברך **אלקים חיים נותן חיים לדבקים בו**, ואין לנמצאים מצד עצמם דבר כי אם מה שמשפיע להם השי״ת, **ובזה השית׳** אחד ואין זולתו...

לא יבא **החיים לנמצאים רק מצד הדביקות** שיש לנמצאים בו יתברך, ועל ידי חטא נכרת מן הדביקות הזה.

ולפיכך **אצל הדביקות נזכר חיים** שנאמר ואתם הדבקים בד׳ אלקיכם **אלקים חיים**, וזה מפני **שהדביקות גורם החיים** כי הוא יתברך נקרא עיקר...וידוע כי האילן והענפים כאשר דביקים בעיקר יש להם חיים מן העיקר ואם נבדל הגוף מן העיקר מיד אין לו חיים, וזהו פי׳ הכתוב כי **עץ חיים** היא למחזיקים בה, וזה כי על ידי התורה הוא דבקות האדם בבוראו, **ודבר זה מבואר** בכמה מקומות **למעלה....**

One of these passages which Maharal alludes to is in the comment on *Avot* 1:12, pp. 151-153, where in context of discussing how תורה ״עי״ התורה יש לו דביקות בו ית׳, the way of is inextricably linked, even identified, with קבלה and שפלות, leading to *devekut*.

[58]*Derek Hayim*, p. 65

דרך ארץ הוא תוכחות מוסר, וכל דברי מוסר־שלא ילך האדם אחר תאות גופו וחומרו אשר **בו דבק המיתה.**

[59]*Derek Hayim*, p. 265, comment on *Avot* 2:14

ויש לך לדעת כי המיתה מגעת אל האדם כאשר הוא סר מן האמצע אשר נברא האדם עליו ונוטה אל אחד הקצוות, בזה מגיע אל האדם המיתה, ודבר זה מבואר שכל מיתה הוא **קצה**, אבל השווי והאמצע הוא החיים.

[60]Ibid., comment on *Avot* 5:21, p. 630

אחר שסדר צד שמאל...רצד ימין...סדר האמצעי בין שתי הקצוות.

[61]*Derek Hayim*, pp. 225-268.

[62]Ibid., pp. 254-255.

[63]Ibid., p. 266.

ופירשנו הדבר בבחינות שונות זה מזה כדי להעמיד אותך על נכון, כי אף אם הבחינות שונות הכל שורש אחד אמתי, אין ספק בזה כלל למי שמבין

[64]Ibid., p. 102

הנבראים נבראו בשביל שיש בהם הטוב ואם לא היה בנמצאים הטוב לא היו נבראים, כי הדבר שאינו טוב בעצמו אין ראוי שיהיה לו המציאות...קיום העולם ועמידת כל הנבראים הוא מפני שנמצא בהם הטוב, ואם לא היה. נמצא בנבראים הטוב לא היה ראוי להם הקיום, ומפני זה חתם בכל בריאה ובריאה במעשה בראשית וירא אלקים כי טוב.

[65]Pp. 103-104.

ולא נמצא בפי' בכתוב אצל האדם טוב רק ברמז "והנה טוב מאד" ואמרו במדרש מאד זה אותיות אדם. וזה נראה כי האדם חסר ועיר פרא אדם יולד. ואחכ' מתעלה האדם אל המדריגה עד שהוא טוב, ולפיכך צריך האדם לקנות מעלת הטוב ומה שהאדם הוא טוב...היינו כשהוא טוב בעצמו

See also the cognate discussion in *Tif'eret Yisrael*, ch. 12, where themes from *Derek Hayim* and the *Sermon* for *Shabbat ha-Gadol* are conjoined.

[66]The letters for the Hebrew word for man (א-ד-ם) are identical with the word for power (מ-א-ד). See the discussion which follows on the meaning of this identity.

[67]"Derush l'Shabbat ha-Gadol," *Derashot Maharal mi-Prague* (Jerusalem, 1968), pp. 53-54.

האדם נקרא מה מצד...שאין בו דבר...ולפיכך השית' שכינתו את דכא...ומצד הזה האדם הוא מאד, כי אדם במספר מאד, כי מצד שהש"י שוכן שכינתו את דכא ומגביהה הדכא האדם הוא מאד, ומצד עצמו אינו דבר רק השית' נותן לו כח וַהכל הוא מן השית, וזהו ענין האדם כאשר ידע האדם מדרגתו, כי הוא מה מצד עצמו והוא מאד מצד השית' אשר לו כח גדולה וגבורה ורוממות.

[68]See the passage covered by notes 64 and 65.

[69]Ibid., p. 77:

כאשר האדם חזר בתשובה הביא שור שאין לו אלא קרן אחד במצחו **שהוא באמצע**, אחר שהיה האדם נמשך אחר שני קרנות של בהמה אשר **הם נוטים לימין ולשמאל** חוץ מן האמצע, ועזב הקרן שהוא

באמצע...ולכן הביא אל כפרתו שור שהיה לו קרן אחת במצחו שהוא
באמצע...כי הקרן הזה שהוא קרן אמתי, ועם כי הוא גבהות ורוממות
באמת הוא מביא אל השפלות...משפיל עצמו **בתכלית השפלות**, כי
יאמר **מה אני** כי עם החכמה היא הענוה והשפלות.

While the term אמצע or מיצוע—identified with ישר and שווי
as the ideal state—is frequently employed by Maharal, its
definition is not spelled out. This passage is valuable in
providing a context from which the meaning may be
unraveled. The sense of "תכלית השפלות," "מה אני," etc.
makes the linkage of this term with ישר intelligible: both
terms express reconciliation to one's lapses and a resultant sense of total dependence on the divine.

[70]Comment on *Avot* 1:16, p. 173.

וכאשר ברא השי'ת את העולם ברא אותו באמת, כמו שתקנו חכמים
בברכה פועל אמת שפעולתו אמת, כי אין בבריאתה שקר וכמ'ש הכתוב
סמוכים לעד לעולם עשוים באמת וישר

[71]Naḥmanides' comment on Genesis 2:9. For a discussion of its implication see my article "R. Azriel and
Naḥmanides: Two views of the Fall of Man," in *R. Moses
Naḥmanides: Explorations in His Literary Virtuosity* (Harvard University Press, 1984).

[72]See note 70,

כמו שתקנו חכמים בברכה פועל אמת שפעולתו אמת.

[73]*Derek Hayim*, p. 255.

[74]The comment, ibid., reads:

כי אלו ג' דברים מוציאים את האדם מן העולם, שהרי כאשר ברא
השית' את עולמו, כתב בכל אחד ואחד כי טוב ואלו ג' דברים הם רעים
הפך הבריאה שברא הקבה'.

[75]This is one of the ways Maharal evokes the movement
from חמר to צורה. If חמר be "closed" and impervious (as in
end of second introduction to *Gevurot ha-Shem*), צורה is
hollow. The model for this is the tablets (לוחות). See *Derek
Hayim*, comments on *Avot* 6:2, *Avot* 5:7, end, and particularly comment on *Avot* 3:7, pp. 313-314 collated with
Hidushei Aggadot I *(Shabbat)*, p. 80 which relates the צורה
to one in *devekut* (the collation is suggested by Maharal).
P. 669—

ולכן רמז לך הכתוב בצורת אותיות הלוחות אשר הם מורים על ציור השכלי שבתורה המופשט לגמרי, והוא שכל בלא שום צירוף חמרי, בלשון חרות ולא בלשון חקיקה, לומר לך כי התורה היא חירות **וחורין** לגמרי שהצורה היא חירות כמו התבאר...ולפיכך כתב הלוחות נראה משני עבריהם שתהיה החקיקה הזאת חקיקה גמורה והיא צורה לגמרי...ובודאי דבר זה הוא חירות גמור, שאין כאן חמרי לגמרי שבו השעבוד.

חירות is related to חורין לגמרי, in the sense of being perforated; צלם א' is also viewed as צורה in this sense *(Hidushei Aggadot* I [*Shabbat*] p. 80). The "hollowing" process is achieved through קבלה, in the sense explained above.

[76]*Derek Hayim*, p. 263. Throughout Maharal's literary corpus, "right" and "left" are said to be aberrations from the ideal of ישר, שוי, מצע, or, intechangeably, the ideal of "good."

[77]The distinction between גוף and נפש (and their correlatives)—elaborated gradually (בפרקים) throughout *Derek Hayim* and assumed in all Maharal's writing—is already drawn in the Introduction to *Derek Hayim*. Here, גוף is related to gratification (הנאה מחמת יצרו בגופו) p. 68 and is focused on one's self (עצמו), p. 67.

[78]Also in the introduction to *Derek Hayim*, נפש is viewed in terms of the potential harm it may do and its impact on others (היזק לזולתו), p. 68.

[79]A more detailed account of גוף and נפש, cast as an interpretation of Maimonides' "division of the soul" in his *Eight Chapters*, is given in *Derek Hayim*, comment on *Avot* 4:25, pp. 487-488, where גוף is associated with need for nutrition and erotic desire. On the relation of self-satisfaction and pride to גוף, see *Netivot Olam* I, *Netiv ha-'Avodah*, ch. 2, beg., concerning prayer for the sake of the body and correlated (as Maharal suggests) with *Netivot Olam* II, *Netiv ha-Ka'as*, ch. 1, p. 237, on שכור. Also, *Netivot Olam* I, *Netiv ha-Din*, ch. 1, pp. 187-188, on גוף as associated with pride.

[80]*Netiv ha-Din*, p. 187; *Tif'eret Yisrael*, ch. 46, p. 141: הערוה היא מן הימין.

[81]*Netivot Olam* II, *Netiv ha-'Anavah*, ch. 4, p. 10:

וזה שאמר כל מי שיש בו גסות רוח כאלו בא על כל **העריות**, כלומר גס רוח **שמתחבר לעצמו** ואין לו חבור עם אחרים, רק עם עצמו, ובזה דומה כאלו בא על העריות, כי כאשר בא על העריות אין זה רק **החיבור לעצמו** כי הקרובים הם בשר מבשרו ועצמו הם...וזה שהוא גס רוח מתחבר לעצמו בלבד ובזה נחשב שבא על כל העריות.

See the end of n.79.

[82]In *Derek Hayim*, comment on *Avot* 4:25, pp. 487-488, it is associated with such emotions as envy and vindictiveness. For an account of envy as the most corrosive of "left impulses," see *Hidushei Aggadot* I *(Shabbat)*, pp. 85-86:

ולפעמים אינו חפץ כלל באותו דבר שיש לזולתו רק שהוא מקנא בזולתו שאינו רוצה שיהיה לזולתו מה שיש לו...ולא תמצא מדה בכל המדות שהוא נחשב יותר בעל העדר, ממי שנמצא בו הקנאה.

[83]*Netivot Olam* II, *Netiv ha-Bushah*, ch. 1, end; ch. 2, beg., pp. 200-201:

p. 200 - מה שישראל הם עזים מורה שהם בעלי נפש, ואין הנפש שלהם מוטבע בחמר

p. 201 - מדת העזות...שאינו מקבל התפעלות מאחר רק הוא עומד בקושי ערפו שלו

[84]For lion and serpent see *Hidushei Aggadot* I *(Shabbat)*, p. 80: הכחות שהם מימין כמו ארי והנחש שהוא משמאל. Concerning ארי see also *Nezah Yisrael*, ch. 55, p. 202. The relevant passage clearly illustrates the structure of Maharal (ישר or ממוצע as the ideal state, "right" or "left" as aberrations) if we bear in mind the need to collate Maharal's "פרקים":

וכאשר אין האדם צדיק ואינו מקבל כח מן השי״ת אז הארי גובר, כי כח האדם ממוצע ואינו יוצא מן הממוצע, שכל היוצא מן הממוצע הוא טמא הוא רע.

ממוצע, we have seen, is equated with שווי and ישר (this very chapter uses these terms interchangeably). It is a state of being reconciled, in which one senses that one "receives" power from the divine, reminiscent of *Derek Hayim* 1:12 (p. 151): ואין האדם מקוים בו יתברך, ועצם החיות בעצמו הוא אך הקבלה שמקבל, as we learn from the phrase in *Hidushei Aggadot*, is a "right" distraction involving pride and

self-satisfaction which vitiates ישר (see comment on *Avot*
2:2). An aberration from מיצוע is רע (as *Derek Hayim* 1:12
indicated) and טמא (as *Hidushei Aggadot* III *Bava Mezia*,
p. 45, showed). Furthermore, the phrase preceding the
text in *Nezah Yisrael*, under consideration, is:

וכאשר האדם בשלימותו כתוב ומוראכם וחתכם על כל חית הארץ,

וכאשר אין האדם צדיק ואינו מקבל כח מן השית' וכו'

The juxtaposition demonstrates that שלימות consists in
being reconciled to אַיִן, when one "receives."

This very passage in *Nezah Yisrael* uses "heat" (p. 203)
in apposition with lion, which indicates that it too is on
the right ("cold" being therefore on the left). For a passage presuming heat and cold as right and left see *Gur
Aryeh* on Deuteronomy, pp. 49-50.

Love and fear are cast as right and left in *Derek Hayim*
(comment on *Avot* 1:13, end, p. 159 and *Avot* 1:5, end, pp.
129-130); water and fire, too (in *Derek Hayim* comment
on *Avot* 5:1, pp. 605, 608).

Other modes of evoking right and left are שמים and ארץ
with בית המקדש באמצע (*Gur Aryeh* on Genesis, pp. 158-
160); גן עדן and גיהנם (*Derek Hayim*, comment on *Avot*
5:21, p. 630) with בית המקדש באמצע; ח'מר and צורה; אשה
and איש (*Gur Aryeh* on Genesis, p. 31). Awareness of the
meaning of these motifs—and each couplet adds nuances
to the central notion—enables the reader to find his way
in the text and to see Maharal as a uniform and consistent
writer.

[85]*Derek Hayim*, comment on *Avot* 1:12 identifies יצר
הרעwith the "right," hence with גוף; *Netivot Olam* II, *Netiv
Ahavat ha-Shem*, ch. 1, p. 40, views יצר הרע as connected
with נפש. Evidently, if רע involves both "right" and "left"
impulses, so does יצר הרע.

[86]*Derek Hayim*, comment on *Avot* 3:1, p. 277:

ויצר הרע מתגבר באדם מכח גבהות הלב, וכל תאוה וכל קנאה וכיראצא
בו מן הדברים אשר הם גורמים שיבא לידי חטא מתחדשים מכח גבהות
הלב.

As in note 9, יצר הרע implies both גוף (תאוה, as in introduction to *Derek Hayim*) and נפש (קנאה).

[87]This equation is frequent. A telling example is in *Derek Hayim*, comment on *Avot* 2:2, p. 199:

יצר הרע הוא השטן הוא מלאך המות כמו שאמרו בפ׳ק דבבא בתרא **והיצר הרע שנתן באדם הוא עצמו**: השטן והמלאך המות שמביאים האדם אל ההעדר והמיתה

Since the equation of יצר הרע and שטן or מלאך המות is established in the previous phrase, the repetition and emphasis in the second phrase is superfluous—unless we take עצמו in the sense of one's self; עצמו and שטן would then be read in apposition. Maharal defines יצר הרע as including both right and left aberrations from the center, which is *devekut*. He can then proceed to speak of self, in the sense of "right" and "left" (see end of this note), as distracting impulses—שטן—which discourage *devekut* or שווי.

This sense of עצמו as one's self is borne out by the rest of the sentence:

והיצר הרע הוא עצמו: השטן והמלאך המות שמביאים האדם אל ההעדר והמיתה.

We recall that מיתה is synonymous with קצה (comment on *Avot* 2:14, p. 265) and חסרון or העדר as the lack of "good."

The passage continues:

ולפיכך כל זמן שלא יצא האדם לאויר העולם שלא נשלם והוא מתנועע אל ההשלמה, אין דבק בו ההעדר...אבל תכף שננער מבטן אמו והוא נמצא בפעל בשלימות ואינו עומד אל הוי׳ עוד, אז דבק בו ההעדר שהוא יצה׳ר הוא שטן הוא מלאך המות שדבק בכל הנמצאים

On the meaning of עומד אל היוה, see nn. 117, 118, below. On "עצמו" as consisting of "right-left" impulses, see *Derek Hayim*, p. 262:

ויש באדם ג׳ בחינות, הבחינה האחת מצד כחות נפשו, הבחינה השני׳ מצד כחות גופו, הבחינה השלישית, **מצד האדם עצמו** כי אין אלו חלקים בלבד, לכך הבחינה הג׳ **מצד שהוא אדם** כולל **הגוף והנפש שיש** לאדם...**האדם בעצמו**...הוא כולל חלקיו.

[88]See, for example, *Netivot Olam* II, *Netiv ha-'Avodah*, ch. 2, beg. The chapter is concerned with a prayer stance

which is overly נוטה אל ענין הגוף ביותר :גופני, yet the prayer is expressed as שופך נפשו בתפלתו. גוף and נפש in this context are not intended as opposites: both are engaged in an activity which is גשמי, the prayer of שכור.

Correlated to this passage (by the Maharal) is *Netiv ha-Ka'as*, ch. 1, p. 237. It is concerned with התפעלות, a function of גשם, related to שכור (גופני) as well as to כעס (p. 236, נפשי). The concern of *Netiv ha-Ka'as* is not to contrast right and left, but to focus on their common trait —חמריות or גשמיות.

[89]*Hidushei Aggadot* I *(Ketubot)*, p. 159.

[90]See, for example, note 53.

[91]*Hidushei Aggadot* III *(Bava Mezia)*, pp. 19-20.

כל מי שהוא מתיירא מן הדבר בא לאותו דבר...וכאשר הוא מתירא מן העניות הוא נותן לעניות קיום בפועל ובא לו הדבר...ואשר יגרתי יבא לי, כאשר הוא ירא מן דבר אחד והוא **בעצמו** נוטה לפול לפני אותו דבר שהוא ירא ממנו, הנה הוא **מקבל** אותו דבר, ובפרט העניות שהוא העדר בלבד, וכאשר נותן עצמו שהוא קרוב אל ההעדר, מקבל ההעדר שרודף אחריו

[92]*Netivot Olam* II, *Netiv ha-Bitahon*, ch. 1, p. 231:

דכיון שאין בך בטחון אתה גורם ליסורים שיבאו, ועוד כי הפחד גורם שיבאו יסורים על עצמו, כי הכלי אשר הוא שלם וחזק בעצמו אין צריך שיהיה ירא מן השבירה כאשר הוא חזק, אבל כאשר הוא רע[!] קל הוא השבירה, וזה שהוא **מפחד מוכח שאינו שלם** והוא כמו כלי רעוע, שאמר פחד פחדתי ויאתיני מפני שהוא כלי מרועע בשביל הפחד

[93]*Netivot Olam* II, *Netiv Ahavat ha-Shem*, ch. 1, p. 43:

כאשר בא דבר מה על האדם שהוא נראה רע והוא בוטח בו ית' השי"ת מהפך אותה לטובה מצד הבטחון בו יתברך.

לעמול בתורה[94]

[95]*Derek Hayim*, comment on *Avot* 1:12, p. 152.

ופרוש דלא מוסיף שאינו יגע ועמל בתורה אע"ג שלמד התורה רק שאינו עמל בדבר, ואינו מגביר השכל על החומר שדבק בו ההעדר, ולפיכך הוא יסיף.

[96]*Derek Hayim*, comment on 3:16, p. 356:

התורה היא סדר מסודר מן השי"ת אשר גזר השי"ת הסדר כפי חכמתו...הסדר המושרל שהוא התורה.

See also *Netivot Olam* I, *Netiv ha-Torah*, ch. 1, beg. This
סדר is to be correlated to the סדר נבדל elaborated in the
second introduction to *Gevurot ha-Shem*; and this sense
of Torah is spelled out in the following text, *Netiv Ahavat
ha-Shem*, ch. 2, p. 47:

הנסים בודאי הם בשביל התורה לפי שהתורה היא אלקית **והיא על**
הטבע ומנהגו של עולם ודוחה התורה הטבע

The latter passage is an interpretation of *Berakot* 20a,
where a mode of "Torah study" results in transcendence
of nature.

[97]Ibid. *(Derek Hayim).*

[98]Ibid.:

והביאו ראיה לזה איך השכל פועל בגשם כי כאשר יניח האדם לוח
שאינו רחב על נהר אחד כאשר היה אדם עובר עליו, **שמחשבת הנפילה**
גורמת כי תצא הנפילה אל הפעל הרי כי המחשבת פועלת שיצא הדבר
אל הפעל, וכמה דברים **שהמחשבה פועלת**, ומכל שכן **הסדר המושכל**
העליון הוא התורה אשר מתחייב מן השית׳ שהיה פועל כפי סדר
המושכל הזה.

There is an almost identical formulation in *Hidushei
Aggadot* III *(Bava Mezia)*, p. 20, in the passage describing
the mentality of fear.

[99]One who is trusting—בטוח בד׳—is צער הזמן or בלי זמן.
See *Netivot Olam* II, *Netiv ha-Bitahon*, ch. 1, p. 232. A
collation of some of the passages in Maharal's writing
which employ the term מעל הזמן (apparently an original
coinage for this "order") is found in Pardes, *Perakim*, pp.
47-54.

[100]*Netivot Olam* II, *Netiv ha-Ahavah*, ch. 1, p. 42:

דבר זה [רע] מצד המקבלים הם בני אדם **ואינו רע מצד השית׳**...ומאחר
שהטוב והרע שניהם מן התחלה אחת יש לברך על הרע כמו על
הטוב...ואף אצל המקבל שהוא רע **בעצמו**, מכל מקום הוא טוב...
מכל מקום הוא טוב .vs שהוא רע בעצמו is a contrast between
what is considered good by the divine as against what a
person's perceptions view otherwise: (שהוא רע בעצמו).

[101]*Netiv ha-Bitahon*, ch. 1, p. 234:

שאף שרואים וחושבים כי כבר אבדה תקותם אל יתיאש רק יהיו
בוטחים בו עדי עד כי השי׳ת יכול להושיע אותם, וכאשר שם בטחונו בו,

אז על השית' להציל אותו כאשר שם בטחונו בו יתברך לכך נחשב זה מלחמות השית'

[102]*Berakot* 33b, הכל בידי שמים חוץ מיראת שמים

[103]*Ketubot* 30a, הכל בידי שמים חוץ מצינים פחים

[104]*Gur Aryeh* on Deuteronomy, pp. 49-50.

[105]Compare this account from *Gur Aryeh* with a complementary one in *Netivot Olam* II, *Netiv ha-Yir'ah,* ch. 1, pp. 21-23.

[106]While this is Maharal's account, it is reminiscent of Maimonides' *Guide* III:51:

הלא בארתי לך שזה השכל אשר שפע עלינו מהאלה יתברך הוא הדבוק אשר בינינו ובינו, **והרשות נתונה לך**: אם תרצה לחזק הדבוק הזה – תעשה, ואם תרצה להחלישו מעט מעט עד שתפסקהו – תעשה, ולא יתחזק זה הדבוק רק בהשתמשך בו באהבת הא־לוה ושתהיה כונתך אליה וחלשתו תהיה בשומך מחשבתך בדבר זולתו

Whether one will sruggle to maintain *devekut* (transposed to Maharal: rising to the "fear of heaven") or be diverted by thoughts other than the divine ("heat or cold" in Maharal's terms; and more generally, for Maimonides והרשות נתונה לך is one's choice: (בשומך מחשבתך בדבר זולתו). For Maimonides, too, *devekut* entails a state beyond the accidents of nature (much of *Guide* III:51 is devoted to this correlation).

[107]*Derek Hayim*, comment on *Avot* 3:17, pp. 360-361:

והתבאר לך כי הידיעה בטוב ורע הגיע לו מצד שהוא **ברשות עצמו**, ואינו פונה אל עלתו שהוא הטוב ואין כאן רע.

As long as one turns to His Cause (עלתו)—and relates one's experiences to Him—there is no evil. Knowledge of good *and evil*, acquired after the fall, is a consequence of Adam's being ברשות עצמו. This phrase, ברשות עצמו, may be translated as a) an autonomous being, but also b) given to his own perceptions of reality. We have already encountered several phrases which exhibit the meaning of עצמו. The two meanings are of course linked. A "return" to the Cause (לעלתו), i.e., being in *devekut*, entails a denial of perceptions "right" and "left" which divert one from

the "center" of *devekut*. The sense of autonomy is anti-
thetical fo *devekut*.

The passage continues:

ודבר זה ג׳כ מה שהרשות נתונה להיות האדם **בבחירתו** הוא מצד
שהאדם נברא בצלם אלוקים והוא יחיד בתחתונים וגרם לו דבר זה
להיות כא׳ יודע טוב ורע. ואם שאין הדבר הזה לטובתו **כי יותר טוב**
שיהיה ברשות העלה ולא היה בעל בחירה שאפשר לו לעשות הרע
הלא ג׳כ דבר זה מה שהוא כאלקים יודע טוב ורע אינה גכ׳ מעלה אל
האדם כי לאדם אין זה מעלה,
רק שהגיע לו דבר זה מצד שהאדם נברא בצלם אלקים ולכך נעשה
כאלקים יודע טוב ורע
וכך הוא דבר זה מה שהאדם ברשות עצמו להיות בחירתו בבחירתו שיש לו
דמיון אל העלה אעג׳ שאינו לטובתו והבן הדברים

As we saw earlier, too, endowment with the "image of
God" enables one to leap to a "second world," i.e., to
deny the apparent evil one perceives in the mundane.
"Knowledge of good *and evil*" is not to one's own advan-
tage, for from man's point of view, the desirable ideal
would have been to enjoy the bliss of the divine, without
apprehension of a non-divine reality (ידיעת הרע). Knowledge of evil was, however, given to Adam in order that it
be transcended. Autonomy was granted in order that it be
offered up "for the sake of heaven."

[108]The image of being "locked" into the realm of the
natural and material order, rather than sharing in the
"openness" of the עולם נבדל, is employed by Maharal in
the second introduction to *Gevurot ha-Shem*, p. 18, con-
cluding his discussion of miracles:

הנביאים על ידי שהי׳ דבקים בעולם הנבדל היו פותחים **שער הננעל**
הוא עולם הטבע אשר נגעל בעד בעלי הגשם, והם פתחו **שערים**
הסגורים ונכנסו אל עולם הנבדל והביאו מן העולם הנבדל דבר שלא
יתכן לפי הטבע

This imagery is especially poignant in the discussion of
אונאת דברים which figures in *Netiv Ahavat Re'a*, ch. 2, pp.
56-61, *Hidushei Aggadot* III *(Bava Mezia)*, pp. 25-28, and
Perushei Maharal l'Aggadot ha-Shas (Jerusalem, 1958),

pp. 123-131. See, for example, aforementioned *Perushei Maharal*, pp. 130-131:

כך מקובלני מבית אבי אבא כל השערים ננעלו חוץ משערי אונאה (במ'
נט :). כבר אמרנו לך, כי אונאה מפני שהוא עושה את חבירו פחות שאינו
נחשב לכלום, דבר כזה הוא פעולה גמורה שעושה בחבירו **ואין כאן
נעילה, כי הנעילה** ההיא באה מצד אשר המעשה **נתלה** בדבר גשמי, ויש
לדבר גשמי נעילת שער. אבל דבר כזה שהוא לצורה אנושית אינו **תולה**
בדבר גשמי לכך אין בזה נעילת שער.

Here the contrast between נעילה (or לתלות בגשמי) on the one hand, and לתלות בעילה, on the other, emerges clearly. If verbal abuse to which one is subjected (whereby one is considered as "nothing") is "hung" on (נתלה), or related to, mundane causes (דבר גשמי), "the gates are locked" (יש לדבר גשמי נעילת שער). But if the provocation is viewed as leading to צורה אנושית (identified with צלם א', in *Hidushei Aggadot* I, *Shabbat*, p. 80), and is therefore not perceived as temporal, there is no "locking of gates" and one has access to the divine through experience of אין (אינו כלום), focused on the divine.

[109]*Hidushei Aggadot* III *(Bava Mezia)*, p. 32, col. 2.

[110]See, for example, *Netivot Olam* II, *Netiv Ahavat Re'a*, ch. 2, p. 56. In light of the aforementioned usage of נעילה and its relation to דבר גשמי (employed throughout in texts mentioned in n.108), the following passage becomes meaningful:

והטעם אשר נראה לי מה שאמר באונאת דברים ויראת מאלקיך, כי
שערי אונאה לא ננעלו, והוא דבר שלא נמסר ביד שליח רק ביד הקבה'
כמו שנאמר בסמוך ["הנפש אשר בו האונאה בידו של הקבה"] לפיכך
נאמר **ויראת מאלקיך שהוא ביד ד' ואינו ביד השליח**, ומי שהוא עובר
עליו הרי אינו ירא מד' אחר שהוא ביד ד'

In this passage, Maharal reads ויראת מאלקיך in Leviticus 25:17 (ולא תונו...ויראת מאלקיך) as addressed to the one being abused; he should not relate the experience to the שליח. For if the "gates are not locked," the abuse did not originate with the apparent perpetrator, but with the divine:

כי שערי אונאה לא ננעלו והוא דבר שלא נמסר ביד שליח רק ביד הקבה'
כמו דנאמר בסמוך, לפיכך נאמר ויראת מאלקיך שהוא ביד ד' ואינו ביד
השליח, ומי שהוא עובר עליו הרי אינו ירא מד' אחר שהוא ביד ד'.

Relating the "fear" to the "messenger" ignores the ultimate source; by connecting with the center—ויראת
מאלקיך—rather than the periphery, the experience
becomes "fear of heaven."

This meaning is reinforced in the next paragraphs (p.
57), where reference is made to *Netiv ha-Din* in the sense
of קבלת הדין, as explained earlier (n.12):

ובדבר זה לא שייך נעילה בדין כלל כי הדין הוא לפני הקבה' כמו
שתוכל להבין מן הדברים אשר נתבאר בנתיב הדין כי המשפט לאלקים
עש'. ומפני כי מי שהוא מאנה את חבירו אינו מחשיב אותו למציאות
כלל רק כאילו אינו דבר כלל ועושה בו דבר שהוא דין גמור עי' אונאה
זאת...**ודבר זה גורם שאין השער ננעל כלל אבל הוא פתוח לפני השית'
כאשר החטא במדת הדין.**

See also *Nezah Yisrael*, ch. 14 end, p. 85, where it is made
clear that God's censure is implemented by people:

וזה לא שמקולל החוטא מן השית' אשר הוא חוטא אליו, רק כי הבריות
מקללין אותו עד שהוא מקולל מעליונים ותחתונים.

But the purpose is to create *devekut* (p. 86):

ובשביל כך כאשר יסורין באים עליהם מסלק מהם החטא, ועיז' יש להם
דבקות אל השית'

חֵטְא in the last reference refers to חסרון or העדר, in the
sense we saw earlier, an aberration to right or left. This
usage of חטא is frequent. For a definition see, for example, *Derek Hayim*, comment on *Avot* 1:15, end (p. 164):

וזהו שאמר שהוא מביא חטא שהחטא הוא חסרון, כי כל לשון חטא
בכל מקום חסרון כמו...אנכי אחטנה...ולפיכך המרבה דברים בא לידי
חטא וחסרון, בפרט כאשר החסרון הוא בדבר נמשך אחר כח גופני.

[111]"Fear of heaven" in this sense is *devekut*. See *Netiv
Yir'at ha-Shem*, ch. 6, p. 37, col. 1:

כי האדם במספר כ"ל וכאשר חסר לו ההא שמורה על שהוא מיוחד אז
מספרו מה כי מה הוא. וכאשר יש בו יראת שמים והוא האדם, אז הוא
כל.

On "כל" as "ענין אלקי" (in the *Kuzari*'s sense of שכינה) see
Gur Aryeh on Deuteronomy, pp. 31-33.

The relationship between *devekut* and divine sustenance (קיום or חיים) and arresting or "silencing" impulses
from "right" or "left" (עצמו) is expressed in various
modes.

See, in particular, the passage cited at the end of n. 113.
עמל בתורה is understood as מגביר השכל על החומר, and
that makes *devekut* possible: ע״י התורה של אדם הדביקות בו
ית׳ (*Derek Hayim*, p. 152). On multifaceted meanings of
the term "Torah" (which Maharal assumes and develops
further), see G. Scholem, "Meaning of Torah in Jewish
Mysticism," *On the Kabbalah and its Symbolism* (New
York, 1978), pp. 32-86. The comment on *Avot* 3:6 (*Derek
Hayim*, p. 306) also begins with:

על ידי התורה יש לו דביקות עם השית׳

and goes on to state:

**שאין לך בן חורין אלא שעוסק בתורה, מפני שעוסק בתורה מתעלה על
העולם הגשמי** כי השכל מתעלה על העולם הגשמי ומפני זה הוא בן
חורין מן הנהגת העולם הטבעי ומן המלכיות

In commenting on the passage from *Gittin* 7a (cited in
text), Maharal says:

ואין אל מה שאמר השכם והערב עליהן לבית המדרש רמז בכתוב רק
שהכתוב אומר **שידום לד׳**, לצפות ולקוות אל השית׳ כי הוא ילחום
מלחמתו, ודבר זה אינו רק שהוא בוטח בו יתברך...על השכל,
וההשכמה לבית המדרש ללמוד תורה גב׳ אל השכל.

דומיה לד׳ is here linked with לימוד תורה in the above-
mentioned senses, and this linkage is pursued in the
comment on *Avot* 3:3 (p. 294). Commenting on

ומנין שאפלו אחד שיושב ושונה מעלה עליו הכתוב כאלו קיים כל
התורה כולה שנאמר ישב בדד **וידום** כי נטל עליו.

Maharal relates עמל בתורה עסק to גזרת השית׳
אשר גזר על האדם. While this is related to *Tif'eret Yisrael*,
ch. 6, Maharal is here concerned with גזירות as "happen-
ings" to which one is reconciled (p. 294):

ואמר אחכ׳ ישב בדד **וידום** כי נטל עליו כלומר כאשר יושב יחיד, ומקבל
עליו גזירת השית׳ וזהו העול וזהו קביעת השכר, וכן תמצא אצל אהרן
שכתוב וידום אהרן שקבל מדת השית׳ **בדמימה**, ומיד׳ קבל שכר כמו
שדרשו...לפי שהושוו **בדמימה**, שקבלו גזירת המקום באהבה.

The reference is to *Sifra* on Leviticus 11:1-2. דומיה or קבלת שכר and leads to קבלת גזירת המקום באהבה is דמימה. This שכר is explained here as being with שכינה, and in the comment on *Avot* 2:1 as *devekut*.

Maharal's treatment of the *Sifra* is valuable in shedding light on the sense in which he employs the term שווי. שווי—identified with ישר and מיצע as the ideal state—is frequently employed by Maharal, but its definition is not spelled out (see n.69). Maharal's interpretive citation of the midrashic phrase as well as the context helps unravel the meaning of the term.

Maharal's full citation of the *midrash* (ibid., p. 294) is as follows:

וכן תמצא אצל אהרן שכתוב (ויקרא י:ג) וידום אהרן שקבל מדת השי׳
בדמימה, ומיד קבל שכר כמו שדרשו (ספרא) שלכך אמר אחריו (ויקרא
יא:יא)וידבר ד׳ אל משה ואל אהרן לאמר אליהם אמר שיאמרו לאלעזר
ולאיתמר או אינו אלא לאמר לישראל, כשהוא אומר דברו אל בני
ישראל, הרי ישראל אמור מה אני מקיים לאמר אליהם לבניו לאלעזר
ולאיתמר דברו אל בני ישראל לפני **שהושוו בדמימה** שקבלו גזירת
המקום באהבה.

This citation is a collation of two separate parts of the *Sifra*: on Leviticus 11:1—

וידבר ד׳ אל משה ואל אהרן לאמר אליהם, לאמר להם לבנים לאלעזר
ולאתמר, או לאמר להם לישראל. כשהוא אומר דברו אל כל עדת בני
ישראל זו דיבור האמור לישראל, הא מה אני מקיים לאמר אליהם
לאמר לבנים לאלעזר ולאיתמר

and of an earlier passage on Leviticus 10:12—

ויאמר משה אל אהרן ואל אלעזר ואל איתמר בניו, בניו שקולים בו
בכבוד ושקולים בו בדמימה – יכול אף הראשונים שקולים בו בכבוד־
ת׳ל הנותרים שקולים בו בכבוד, ואין הראשונים שקולים בו בכבוד.

Maharal modifies the word שקולים, rendering it הושוו, and in his formulation לפי שהושוו בדמימה שקבלו גזירת המקום באהבה harks back to yet an earlier passage in the *Sifra* on Leviticus 10:3, וידום אהרן:

...כיון ששמע אהרן כך צדק עליו את הדין, שתק, שנאמר וידום אהרון,
ולמודי צדיקים שמצדיקים עליהם את הדין...אברהם צדק עליו את
הדין...יעקב...דוד...

כיון שידע אהרן שבניו ידועי המקום שתק וקבל שכר על שתיקתו, מיכן אמרו כל המקבל עליו ושותק סימן יפה לו, ועל ידי דוד הוא אומר דום לד׳ והתחולל לו...עתים שאדם שותק, עתים...מדבר.

הושיו בדמימה, then, is a term emanating from the sense of being reconciled, evoked in these interpretations of דמימה דומיה. שווי becomes השתוות in the vocabulary of the Baal Shem Tov and R. Mendel of Vitebsk (see Part II, n.57) with a reference to Bahya ibn Paquda's *Hovot ha-Levavot* (gate 10, ch. 6):

שיה׳ שוין בעיניו תהלת בני אדם וגנוים לו, בעשותו רצון ד׳ יתרומם ויתהדר..

[112]*Derek Hayim*, comment on *Avot* 2:2, p. 200:

שני יצר הרע שברא הקבה׳ יצרא דערוה ויצרא דע׳ז.

ערוה was discussed earlier as emanating from the "right"; עבודה זרה stems from the left. See also the cognate "ערוה and חרב" in *Netivot Olam* I, *Netivot ha-Din*, ch. 1, p. 187, col. 2:

יציאה אל שני קצוות, החרב והערוה, אשר ידוע למשכילים

[113]*This sense of* עבודה זרה is frequent. See, for example, *Netivot Olam* I, *Netiv ha-Emet*, ch. 2, p. 200, where "reifying" (נותן מציאות) in the sense that appeared in n.26 is employed. Considering that something "is" when it "is not" ruptures אחדות, creates שניות, and is עבודהזרה.

It is in this context that the comment on R. Eleazar ben Arak's teaching דע מה שתשיב לאפיקורוס״ (*Avot* 2:14, p. 268) is to be understood: his counsel calls for arresting "idolatrous" thoughts:

ודע מה שתשיב לאפיקורוס, דבר זה הוא הרהורי מינות שעולים במחשבת נפשו של האדם...שאם ילמד מה שישיב לאפיקורוס כל שכן שלא יעלה על לבו ומחשבתו שום הרהור רע, ומפני כי הנפש מהרהר המינות אמר שיהי׳ שקוד לבטל זה מעיקרא. והרי זה תקון נפשו ביותר מן כל הראשונים.

The expression "מחשבת נפשו" in this passage is to be noted. The concern is with thoughts flowing from the left-directed נפש, and these thoughts need "to be nullified at their root." The אפיקורוס is associated with יצר הרע,

who militates for deviation from *devekut*, and this "idola-trous" impulse must be arrested.

[114]*Gur Aryeh* on Genesis, p. 239. On the popularity of this passage with nineteenth-century Hasidic masters, see "Mavo," *Perushei Maharal mi-Prague l'Aggadadot ha-Shas* I, eds. M. Kasher and J. J. Blecherowitz (Jerusalem, 1958), pp. 30-31.

[115]*Hidushei Aggadot* III *(Bava Mezia)*, pp. 32-33. A discussion of Rabbinic attitudes to sex is introduced by:

ודבר זה באו להרחיק חכמים ["שחוש המשוש חרפה הוא לנו"] כי לא
יסבול דבר זה הדעת כי יהיה יסוד כל... נבנה על דבר גנאי וחרפה...אין
בחבור איש עם אשתו שום דבר רע כלל...רק שבשביל האדם מכוין
לתאותו ויצרו ומצד הדבר הזה הדבר הוא גנאי כי הוא כלי היצר, ולפיכך
קודם שחטא ונטה אל תאותו ויצרו, אין בזה שום גנאי, רק כאשר נכנס בו
היצר ונתלבש בתאוה חמרית אז הוא גנאי ובזיון ומצד התאוה...ואמר
שנטה אל התאוה אז ראוי היה לכסות בשר ערוה

In order to avoid insinutation of תאוה and יצר, Maharal suggests:

ומאחר כי שמו יתברך מחבר שניהם ועל זה אמר האהבה, שהוא עצם
החבור שהוא מן השית', **דוחה הבשר הגשמי**, שודאי ראוי שיהיה גובר
כח חבור זה על הבשר הגשמי שהוא עומד כנגד זה.
ואידך סבר כי כאיש גבורתו, כי אבר התשמיש יש לו כח איש שזה
האבר הוא עצמו ההבדל בין איש לאשה, נתן לו כח מיוחד שאינו גשמי
כמו שאר האברים, והוא **מושל ודוחה בכח גבורתו** שנתן לו, עד שגומר
פעולתו, שבשביל זה נקרא זה איש.

מתנוע אל השלימות[116].

[117]*Derek Hayim*, comment on *Avot* 2:2, p. 199.

ומי שאינו בשלימות בפעל הנה עומד אל ההשלמה ולא ימשוך אחר זה
חסרון אבל כאשר הוא יושב ונח כאלו הגיע כבר אל ההשלמה וימשוך
אחר דבר זה העדר וחסרון כי אין השלמת דבר בעולם שאין דבק בו
חסרון.

[118]*Derush l'Shabbat ha-Gadol*, pp. 105-106:

מי שהוא דורך אל השלום אין מגיע לו הפסד מפני שהוא דורך אל
השלום. אבל שיהיה בשלום לגמרי דבר זה אינו, ולכך הם בגלות מצד
שאין השלום עמהם לגמרי, אבל הם דורכים אל השלום...מצד שאין
שלימות עמהם לגמרי, אבל עשו וזרעו הוא הפך זה, שאצלו שייך כמו
שהי' כונת דוד שאמר לאבשלום לך בשלום, שהי'כונתו שיהי' השלום

עמו ויהי' בנחת ובשלום לגמרי, כי עשו השלום עמו לגמרי, שהרי מספר
עשו הוא שלום...ולמה מספר של עשו שלום? אך אל יחשוב אדם, כי
דבר זה הוא לטוב לו כמו שלא היה טוב לאבשלום שאמר לו דוד לך
בשלום, כי העולם הזה אין ראוי שיהיה בשלום עתה, רק לעתיד
כשיבא המשיח, כמו שהתבאר למעלה, ועשו אשר שלומו עמו, א'כ אינו
דורך אל השלום שהוא לעתיד...

[119]Talmud *Shabbat* 118b.

[120]*Derek Hayim*, comment on *Avot* 4:19, p. 472:

המתים בדרך מצוה, הנה הוא מתנועע אל השית' נחשב שהוא עם
השית', כי התנועה אל הדבר כאלו הוא אחד עמו מה שאין כך מי
שעשה כבר המצוה וקנה אותה, הרי קנה המדריגה שיש לעושי מצוה,
אבל לא יאמר בזה שהוא מתעלה להתדבק בו יתברך לגמרי, אבל
כאשר הוא מת בדרך מצוה והיה מתעלה להתדבק בו, ומתוך זה הרי
הוא מת, הרי מתדבק עם השי"ת

On the meaning of "death" and its relation to *devekut*
through הודאה, see notes 39, 58, 122, 132, 134.

[121]On the basis of a comment on *Avot* 3:1 (*Derek
Hayim*, p. 283), it is possible to define the relationship
between the ethic regulating the "right-left" poles and
that regulating the "middle" (see ibid., p. 262, where it is
stressed that the "poles" and the "middle" are in need of
their own ethic, מוסר). The ethic of the "poles" elicits a
response of reconciliation to one's lapses; the ethic of the
"middle" relates the state of being reconciled, a sense of
אָין, to the supportive, ultimate cause ישר] (עלתו.(see nn. 7,
17) pertains to both modes. When the terms are differen-
tiated, being עלול refers to the former, הודאה (n. 134)
refers to the latter.

ואמרו דע מאין באת מטפה סרוחה, ולאן אתה הולך למקום עפר רמה
ותולעה, כל הדברים כמו שאמרנו שאין האדם נחשב מצד עצמו
כלל.כאשר מצד התחלתו ומצד סופו אין נחשב לכלום [ראה להלן,
מצד ימין מצד שמאל], הנה האדם בזה הוא עלול לגמרי כאשר אין
נחשב הן מצד התחלתו הן מצד סופו. ועדיין אם אין מסתכל שיש לו
עלה לא היה נכנס תחת רשות העלה, אבל בזה שמקבל עליו השם
יתברך לעלה שיודע שיתן לעתיד דין וחשבון לפניו אז ידע שהוא יתברך
העלה, והאדם הוא עלול לגמרי, ובכל הדברים האלה האדם נכנס תחת
רשות העלה...כי ע"י. שיסתכל בשלשה דברים אלו אין לו הסרה מן

השית' **לא לימין ולא לשמאל** והוא מקושר עם השית' ובזה אינו בא ליד חטא, והבן הדברים האלו מאד.

The term חטא at the end of the passage is used in the sense of aberration to right or left. See n.110.

[122]Comment on *Avot* 2:14, p. 264:

ואחכ' אמר ושוב יום אחד לפני מיתתך, ור'ל שאם חטאת ואין צדיק בארץ אשר יעשה טוב ולא יחטא יהיה נזהר לעשות כל יום ויום תשובה. ובשביל זה יהיה לו חיי עוה'ב בשלימות

See also comment on *Avot* 2:10, pp. 251-252; comment on *Avot* 4:19, p. 472; *Netivot Olam* II, *Netiv ha-Teshuvah*, ch. 2, p. 151, where the phrase שוב יום א' לפני מיתתך is interpreted:

כי עיקר תשובה קודם וסמוך למיתתו ולא שישוב זמן הרבה קודם מיתתו, וזה מפני כי **האדם במיתתו ראוי לשוב אל השית'**, ולפיכך אם שב קודם מיתתו, אז **במיתתו שב אל השי'ת לגמרי**

This passage stresses how a psychological or spiritual "death" is a suitable occasion to struggle for "return" to the ultimate Cause. See end of n. 120 for analogous usages of "death."   [123]See n.69.

[124]See n.86, on *Avot* 3:1. Maharal there goes on to develop this notion further:

שיצר הרע מסית האדם עד שהוא מביא את האדם לידי אבוד, לכך אין גרוי והסתה רק כאשר יחשוב האדם עצמו במדריגה עליונה מאד ואז יצר הרע מסית אותו עד שהוא מפיל אותו ומאבד אותו לגמרי.

[125]See *Derek Hayim*, p. 207; *Neẓah Yisrael*, p. 15, very beg. of ch. 3.

[126]Ibid. Following the above (n.124), Maharal writes:

אבל כאשר **רוחו ולבו** נשבר בקרבו אין כאן יצר הרע שיהי' מסית את האדם להפילו ולאבדו.

When, as a result of failure, one's רוח (identified with גוף, comment on *Avot* 4:25, p. 486) and לב (identified with נפש, comment on *Avot* 2:11, p. 255) are neutralized, there is no יצר הרע; for if one does not resent the sense of אַין there is potential for *devekut*.

On divinely ordained סבות as a deterrent to falling, see comment on *Avot* 2:4, p. 207; *Hidushei Aggadot* III

(Sanhedrin), pp. 236-237, statement beginning "Rav Ashi."

[127]An extensive discussion of this theme in *Tif'eret Yisrael*, ch. 48, pp. 146-151.

[128]*Hidushei Aggadot* III *(Sanhedrin)*, p. 251, col. 2, bottom; p. 252, col. 1. Maharal's account of *Sanhedrin* 106a, which deals with David's "trial."

[129]*Netivot Olam* II, *Netiv ha-Teshuvah*, ch. 4, pp. 155-160. See note on הודאה, n.134.

[130]*Hidushei Aggadot* IV *(Avodah Zorah)*, pp. 28-30.

[131]See n.122, that יום א' לפני מיתתך is used in the sense of "immediately."

[132]*Derek Hayim*, comment on *Avot* 2:14, p. 265. This is the passage covered by n.58. Significantly, this definition of מיתה as aberration from *devekut* appears as comment on *Avot* 2:11, following שוב...לפני מיתתך *(Avot* 2:10). Both *mishnayot* are part of the group *(Avot* 2:8-2:14) which Maharal treats as one thematic unit. See n.60.

[133]On regret as "material," and frustrating *devekut*, see *Hidushei Aggadot* I *(Ketubot)*, p. 159:

באשר האדם הוא בעל חומר ולכן הוא מתחרט על אשר עשה, ודבר זה ידוע כי החרטה הוא **השתנות** מן הן ללאו או מן לאו אל הן וכל שנוי הוא בחומר, ולפיכך מי שאצלו החרטה הוא בעל חומר שאצלו ימצא השנוי בו כי אשר בו מדת השכלי לא יתחרט כלל כי אין חרטה בשכל, ולפיכך אי איתשיל על "שבועתי"

(שבועה is defined in this passage as *devekut*, קיום, p. 80) מורה שהוא מטה אל החומר ואין בעל חומר מקבל הקיום מן השית', ולעולם הוא נשאר אפשרי מפני שהוא בעל שנוי והוא הפך הקיום [דביקות] וגם בעל אפשרות גמור, ודבר שהוא אפשרי מקבל העדר, **ואם הוא אינו מסוגל אל אפשרות מצד עצמו הוא מקבל הקיום ממנו ית' ויוצא מן ההעדר.**

The boldface phrase is most instructive: on conceding one's "impossibility" from the vantage point of one's self, one receives divine קיום and is no longer "lacking," because of being in *devekut*. Contrasted here, in effect, is repentance based on guilt and "return" based on הודאה. See next note.

[134]*Netivot Olam* II, *Netiv ha-Teshuvah*, ch. 5, p. 161:

עיקר התשובה הוא הודאה שהוא מודה על חטאיו. שההודאה מביא
שהשי״ת מקבל אותו בתשובה, כי כאשר מודה על חטאיו מוסר עצמו
אל השי״ת ושב אל השית׳ לגמרי **כי זהו ענין החודאה כמו שבארנו דבר**
זה בכמה מקומות, ואז השית׳ מקבל אותו בתשובה בשביל הודאה זאת
שמוסר עצמו אליו

One of the fullest treatments of הודאה is in *Netivot Olam*
II, *Netiv ha-'Avodah*, ch. 10, beg. See whole discussion
and its epitome in:

אנו נותנים הודאה אל השית׳ שאנו שלו, ואין אנו מצד עצמנו שום דבר,
רק הכל להשם יתברך

And further in ch. 10:

לכך נקרא יום המיתה כריעה — שהאדם בטל חיותו ושב אל העלה,
שהכורע יש לו נפילה על ברכיו ומוסר עצמו אל אשר כורע
אליו...הכריעה במודים למסור נפשו אל השית׳, ושב אל העלה במה
שהוא עלתו...הכריעה...שבזה האדם מבטל עצמו אל השי״ת עד שאינו
נמצא, ולפיכך ראוי שתהי׳ הכריעה בלא זמן רק בפעם אחד...שכל הוית
האדם הוא בזמן, **ובטול בלא זמן כלל**

See also *Derush l'Shabbat ha-Gadol*, p. 93:

במזמור **לתודה**...ר״ל כי אנו מודים אליו יתברך, כי הכל הוא אל השית׳,
הן מצד שבראנו...הן מצד שאחר שבראנו אנחנו אליו, כלומר שאל
תאמר...[ו]אחר שבראנו אין צריכין ח׳ו אליו עוד...על זה אמר **ולו אנחנו**
כי אנו תלויים בו, ואם ח׳ו אינו עושה חסדים עמנו אי אפשר שיכול
האדם לעמוד, וזהו ולו אנחנו בשביל **שאנו תלוים בו**, והנה התודה שיש
בה החמץ הרי החמץ כנגד מה שאמר ולו אנחנו. כי החמץ מורה על יצר
הרע, וצריך האדם שיזבח יצרו ולצאת מן **יצה״ר**

(in the sense Maharal understands it)

ולשוב אל השי״ת ומזה הצד הוא אל השית, שכל אשר הוא שב אל
השית׳ נכנס ברשותו והוא שלו, וקודם שהוא שב אליו נראה כאלו לא
היה ברשותו, אבל מפני השבתו הוא אליו לגמרי, וזהו כנגד בעל
תשובה שזובח יצרו ומתודה עליו ושב אל השית׳.

Also, *Gevurot ha-Shem*, ch. 64, pp. 296-297:

פירוש ענין הודאה ר״ל שהוא **מודה לו ומשלים עצמו** אליו, כי כל מי
שמודה לאחר משלים עצמו אליו שהוא תחת רשותו...שהוא משלים
עצמו ונפשו אל השי״ת...וההשלמה הזאת שהוא משלים עצמו אל
השית׳ הוא הדבקות בו במה שהוא משלים נפשו ומתדבק אל השי״ת,
וכל נמצא לפי מה שהוא מדריגתו יש לו דבקות בו יתברך. ולפיכך יש

לכל נמצא הודאה שהוא השלמה אל השית׳ בפני עצמו.

הודאה, based on these collated sources, is concession of one's total dependence in the wake of a fall. As a result, one gives one's self over to the divine, renouncing a sense of autonomy (suggested in *Netiv ha-'Avodah*, ch. 10, through the contrast of kneeling vs. serpent) and reconciles (משלים עצמו אל) one's self to the need for, and fact of, total dependence (הודאה and השלמה are used in juxtaposition). In such a state one is above time (בלי זמן). [חטאים, here too, are intended in the broader sense described above, n.110, end.]

[135]The most important passages for this theme are *Nezah Yisrael*, ch. 14, p. 83 and *Gur Aryeh* on Numbers, p. 164, col. 1. See also *Netivot Olam* II, *Netiv ha-Bushah*, ch. 1, p. 200, ch. 2, p. 201; *Netivot Olam* II, *Netiv Ahavat ha-Shem*, ch. 1, p. 44.

[136]*Netiv ha-Bushah*, p. 200; *Derek Hayim*, comment on *Avot* 5:21, pp. 628-629, on the passage:

ביצה כה:—מפני מה נתנה תורה לישראל מפני שהם עזים

For a cognate discussion of this pervasive theme—rising to *devekut* from the "death" of failure—see *Perushei Maharal l'Aggadot ha-Shas* IV (Jerusalem, 1967), pp. 78-79:

מלאך המות מצד מה הוא סיבה לדבוק העליון, כי מצד שהגוף נעדר הוא קונה התדבקות במדריגה הנבדלת ולפיכך מלאך המות שהוא כח מפסיד הגוף מגביה ומקרב אותו אל מקום מדריגתו אחר שהמיתה היא העדר הגוף, ועי׳׳ז קונה האדם הדבוק העליון אחר המיתה

Devekut is a result of the הודאה (see n.134) which the "fall" elicits. (On Maharal's usage of "מיתה," see nn. 39, 57).

[137]*Avot* 2:11.

[138]On Maharal's psychological account of anger, see *Derek Hayim*, comment on *Avot* 5:12, pp. 587-588, with passage beginning "ואמנם יש לפרש." The principal point is: מי שהוא נוח לכעוס הוא רב פשע. Maharal's reading of *Nedarim* 22b is "אדם הכועס בידוע שעונותין מרובין," not שעונותיו מרובין מזכיותיו, which is his reading in *Netiv ha-*

Ka'as, ch. 2, p. 238. The abridgment here is intended to emphasize the psychological aspect discussed here. See elaboration of this theme in the rest of the passage; also comment on *Avot* 2:10, p. 251.

[139]Other examples of Maharal's account of Rabbinic statements in terms of the inclination to "project" resentment, see *Netivot Olam* II, *Netiv Lev Tov*, ch. 1, p.210 (bottom)-p. 211 (top); ibid., *Netiv Ahavat Re'a*, ch. 3, p. 62. The comment on *Avot* 2:14 is repeated, ibid.:

כאשר שונא הבריות שהם האדם בכלל כאלו דוחה כל העולם.

[140]See n.111.

[141]The הפכים which need to be bridged are *not* "fire" and "water," as Maharal makes clear in *Derek Hayim*, comment on *Avot* 5:17, p. 609:

ולכן אמר מחלוקת שהיא לשם שמים סופה להתקיים ושאינה לשם שמים אין סופה להתקיים. **שהמחלקת יוצא מן האחדות** והם הפכים (ז.א. החלקים והאחדות), ואין ההפכים נמצאים יחד.

[142]Ibid., p. 606:

המחלוקת שהוא לשם שמים. אף כי המחלוקת מחולק מצד עצמו והם הפכים, וההפכים מצד עצמם אי אפשר שימצאו יחד, אבל מצד השי'ת אשר הוא סבה להפכים – הנה אלו שני הפכים הם אחד, כי הם אל השית' שהוא אחד **ובשניהם עושה ופועל רצונו** מה שירצה הוא יתברך, ולכן אותם הפכים אשר אי אפשר שיהי' יחד, מכל מקום מצד השית שהוא כולל הכל אם הם הפכים הם מתאחדים, וזה אמרם כאן כל מחלקת שהיא לשם שמים סופה להתקיים.
See also *Gur Aryeh* on Deuteronomy, p. 49, beg: ורבותינו דרשו.

[143]Hence **מחלקת לשם שמים**. For a valuable discussion of the relationship between—and definitions of—חלק and (עהין אלקי) כל, See *Gur Aryeh* on Deuteronomy, pp. 30-33.

[144]Ibid, pp. 605-609.

[145]*Gur Aryeh* on Deuteronomy, pp. 49-50. On התייחסות see also *Derek Hayim*, comment on *Avot* 1:2, p. 106. See also *Netivot Olam, Netiv Yir'at ha-Shem*, ch. 1, p. 21 (2nd column).

הכל בידי שמים חוץ מיראת שמים...וחו' שיהי' יראת שמים בידי השית' כי היראה מה שמחשיב עצמו לאין וללא כלום לפני העלה ית'

כמו שהתבאר, ואם היה זה מן השית הי׳ חו׳ בא ממנו דבר שאינו נעשה
מציאות, ובו יתברך נתלה המציאות
("נתלה") in the sense explained earlier [n.108]),
ואף דכתיב ד׳ ממית ומחי׳, ודבר זה ביד השית׳ היינו שמסלק מן האדם
חיים בשביל חטאו, והוא [מצדו = כמתפעל] נעדר לגמרי, אבל לומר
שיהי׳ בידו (ביד ד׳) יראת שמים דבר כזה אא׳ לומר מאחר שעיקר
היראה שמחשיב עצמו עלול, **וזה אינו מצד העלה**, כי כל העדר אינו
מפעולת פועל...אינו מצד העלה, שהרי **מצד העלה הוא נמצא ממנו**,
שלכך נקרא עלה.

In the next paragraph (p. 22), the support of the עלה is
expressed as אהבה.

The upshot of this passage is that the divine has
nothing to do with a negative "interpretation" that the
עלול may place on a situation; but the divine does generate the מציאות or קיום that a reconciled one, עלול, experiences, notwithstanding the apparent lack, העדר. When
"בו ית׳ נתלה המציאות," then "מצד העלה הוא נמצא ממנו. Hence,
the reality of *devekut*:

כי היראה היא מגיע אל עצם אלקותו יתברך...כי היראה היא עצם
האלקות...הוציא יראתו מחיקו שהוא עם עש׳ית לגמרי

In other words, challenged by "מקרים" one's gesture is to
be "תולה בטחונו" (phrase in *Netiv ha-Bitahon*, ch. 1, p. 232
borrowed from *Menahot* 29b; the relating to a "second
world" which the comment suggests is to be correlated
with *Derek Hayim*, comment on *Avot* 3:3, p. 293) and the
resultant transcendence and protection that comes with it
is a divine achievement. (On "תולה," see n.108.)

[146]See note 7.

[147]See note 150; also the correlation of notes 35-37.

[148]*Derek Hayim*, p. 266. ושנאת הבריות היא יציאה מן **האדם**
עצמו שהוא היושר.

[149]See discussion in the beginning of the article.

[150]*Gevurot ha-Shem*, pp. 296-297.

[151]הוא יתברך הישר בעצמו. The phrase is frequent. See, for
example, *Perushei Maharal*, p. 163, which also amplifies
the point at hand:

הכל בידי שמים חוץ מצנים פחים. הקור והחום...הפכים יוצאים אל
הקצה יוצאים מן היושר, ולפיכך אמר שאין ברשות הקב"ה'...**והוא ית'**
היושר בעצמו, ולפיכך אלו שהם הפכים היוצאים מן השווי אל הקצה
לגמרי אינם ביד הקב"ה' ומציאותם הוא מצד שהם נמשכים אחר
הבריאה, אבל שיהיה ביד השי"ת דבר זה אינו...והאחד [במובן אחדות]
הוא יראת שמים, כי יראת שמים הוא מה שהנמצא נחשב לאין כי זהו
יראה שהנמצא נחשב לאין, ואין זה ביד הק'בה.

Correlate with *Derek Hayim*, p. 151:

ואין האדם מקוים בו יתברך [בו = דרכו]...ולפיכך כל אשר הוא משפיל
עצמו [במובן מהר"ל] הוא מקבל הקיום מן השי"ת אשר בו נתלה הכל
[נתלה = על פי הגדרת מהר"ל, 108 .n]

[152]The first usage of עצמו in the *Derek Hayim* passage,
p. 266, is in Maharal's usual sense; in the second usage,
the usual self remains, but divine יושר—during *devekut*
—is in control. Compare *Netiv ha-Ka'as*, ch. 2, p. 239:

כי האדם הוא מסודר עם השית' שהוא עלה לו, וכאשר כועס הוא יוצא
מן הסדר

Devekut (האדם מסודר עם השי"ת) is threatened by the usual
self, eruption of anger. For this reason, this state must be
accompanied by prayer, p. 238, col. 2:

יש צד אף שאינו נוטה אל הקצה יש צד פירוד וסילוק הדביקות כאשר
ראוי לו לבקש הדביקות בו ית', והוא אינו מבקש הדביקות הרי זה פירוד
ממנו, וזה בשעה שיצא שיצא לדרך וצריך האדם אל הדבקות, הוא הלוידה.

[153]*Derek Hayim*, comment on *Avot* 2:9, p. 236:

בודאי מצד הכחות המחולקים מחצה נוטה אל הטוב ומחצה נוטה אל
הרע, אבל מצד האדם אשר הוא כולל כל החלקים יש לאדם נטי' אל
הרע **כי בכלל האדם הוא הרע.**

[154]*Netivot Olam* II, *Netiv Koah ha-Yeẓer*, ch. 4, p. 129.

בודאי יש לאדם לעמוד נגד יצהר' בכל כחו, אבל לא יחשוב כי יכול
להתנגד אליו ולעמוד כנגדו, רק יחשוב שהוא דבר קשה מאוד מאוד
והוא ירא מן יצר הרע, רק **כי הסילוק הזה הוא מצד השית'** אשר הוא
מסלק היצר הרע, אבל האדם כל זמן שנאמר כי הוא בעצמו יכול להתנגד
אליו ולהיות גובר עליו אז היצר הרע גובר עליו בכח.

Chapter 4 in *Netiv Koah ha-Yeẓer* is introduced as
follows:

הענין הזה שיתפלל האדם אל השי"ת תמיד שיסיר את היצר הרע ממנו,
אבל מעצמו קשה הוא. כי האדם נחשב שהוא שבוי ואסור ביד מלך זקן

וכסיל הוא יצה׳ר שנקרא בכל מקום בשם הזה, והרי אין חבוש מתיר
עצמו מבית אסורים, וצריך לאחר להתירו הוא השם ית׳ אשר מוציא
אותו מבית אסורים.

Part II

[1]*Peri Etz*, p. 31.

[2]See Part I, the material covered by nn.57-60, 64-70.

[3]See, for example, ספר ראשית חכמה *Likutei Amarim*
(henceforth, L.A.), p. 13a; ספר עשרה מאמרות L.A., p. 24a;
הספר חובות הלבבות L.A. p. 16b.

[4]See n.1.

[5]*Likutei Amarim*, p. 8a. לעבוד בתמימות

[6]L.A. p. 3a.

[7]L.A. p. 26b:
כל דבר שרואה יאמין באמונה שלימה שהראו לו מלמעלה כדי לזכור
בהקב׳ה — ויפשיט הדבר הזה מגשמיות, דרך משל אם רואה כלי נאה
יאמר מהיכן בא לדבר זה התפארות אם לא ממנו ית׳

[8]L.A. p. 2b: מי הוא זה בכל דבר נרכב וכו׳

[9]והאלקים עשה שייראו מלפניו (Ecclesiastes 3:14) is cited
frequently: see, for example, L.A. p. 5a. The verse is used
in the same way by Maharal.

[10]סוף מדריגה is at עקב - יעקב

[11]L.A. p. 11a; see also L.A. p. 37b:
וישראל צריך להפשיט עצמו עד שיהא יש״ר לא״ל ללמדנו מוסר
בהשגחה לידע שכל שבעולם הוא גילוי אלקותו ית׳ ונמצא איך שיהי
הכל ישר, כי הכל הוא חיות אלקים, וכן כתוב אשר עשה האלקים את
האדם ישר והמה בקשו חשבונות רבים.

[12]L.A. p. 4b on context of ישראל as "ראש-לי".

[13]L.A. p. 3b:
תחלת ההשגה לברוא העולמות היה שייראו מלפניו והנה ההסתכלות
הזה ניתן באדם — כשבאה לו איזו יראה אזי יסתכל בעין שכלו לבחינת
היראה כי באה להשיבה אל מקורה, ויחזור באור חוזר אל היראה
הראשונה שממנה נלקחה שהיא ראשית הדבר וזהו (קהלת ב:יד) החכם
עיניו בראשו, שמסתכל על ראשית הדבר שממנו נלקח.

In L.A. 4b-5a, R. Mendel speaks of moving from יראת
ענש to יראה העיקרית.

[14]L.A., p. 3a.

[15]L.A., p. 3b.

[16]L.A., p. 5a:

וצריך האדם לכנוס למדרגת סבה הראשונה שהיא למעלה מכל הער־
למות המסובבים מאתה ואז הוא בעלמא דחירות.

[17]L.A., p. 5b:

כל הדברים המקרים יתעלו ויתבטלו ממנו בבהירות הרב הזה כיון
שהוא למעלה מהם.

[18]Ibid., להעתיק מחוץ לטבע.

[19]L.A., p. 9a:

העושה חילוק ופירוד, הוא עצמו בפירוד ושבירה.

[20]Ibid., The effort to rise above "nature" requires
struggle — והנה לבוא למדריגה הנ׳ל צריך **יגיעה** להכניעו להחומר —
See *Peri Etz*, p. 17:

וזהו שמזדמנים לו מלחמות וסבות הכל לחזקו ולנסותו אם יעמוד
באמונתו

See also p. 2b on "overcoming" (נצוח) the "left" with the
"right." Engagement with Torah implies subordinating
the perception of evil to a conviction of the good inherent
in the situation, which then materializes:

והנה בתורה יש בחינת ימין ושמאל...הענין שארז׳ל (ברכות ה.) לעולם
ירגיז אדם יצר טוב על יצר הרע שזהו בחינת **נצוח** אז נכלל שמאלא
בימינא, ובאמת כל מה שנשפע על האדם בין טוב ובין רע מן הבוי׳ת...ר־
כשאדם מסתכל היטב רואה שהכל הביא השית׳ לטובתו ללמדו
דעת...ומודה ומבין שבכל דברים יש רחמנות,,,**ואז כשהאדם נוהג כך
נכלל הכל בימין מדת הנצוח** שמנצח על ההיפך

[21]L.A., p. 7a.

והנה אף שהאדם מתעורר עצמו מלמטה ביראה, אלו לא הי׳ הקבה׳
עוזרו לא הי׳ בא לזה.

[22]Ibid.

שבאמת כל זמן שבאדם אהבה או יראה איזו שתהי׳ **כשחוזר אח׳כ
לאהבתו ויראתו של הקבה׳** הוא מהקבה׳; כי גם אה׳ויר רעה שהיתה לו
היא משתלשלת מאה׳ויר העיקרית —ונמצא כששב והחזירה לשרשת
אחז בחבל ההשתלשלות ונמצא היא של עליון.

[23]Ibid.,

אך כשהאדם נופל למטה במדרגה שלמטה שם שום אה׳ויר כגון
להכעיס, נמצא כששב הוא מהתעוררורותו שב, כי כבר נפסק מן החבל
האחוז לחזור בו.

וזהו כל שהעליון יכול לפשוט את ידו, כי ידו אהבה או יראה וכ'ז
שנתפשטות אה'ויר אפ' בקליפות דמלכותו בכל משלה ההתעוררות
הוא של עליון כאמור, והשאר מי שנפל במותרות שלמטה מאה'ויר אז
כששב הוא של תחתון ויובן.

[24]יראת הרוממות, respectively. and יראת העינש

[25]L.A., p. 3b:

יראת העונש...בא במזכרת במחשבתו בלבו לעורר יראת העיקרית וע'י
תתעלה אל שרשה והעונש יתבטל וזהו המתקת הדינין, לא כמו
הכסילים האומרים שאין לשים אל לבם יראת העונש ואם באה
במחשבתם דוחים אותה, לבל תעלה לפניהם כלל, שאכ' במה תתוקן
ואיך ימתיקו הדינין?

[26]*Netivot Olam* II, *Netiv Ahavat ha-Shem*, ch. 1, p. 45.
[27]Maharal's second introduction to *Gevurot ha-Shem*.
[28]עולם נבדל
[29]*Peri Etz*, p. 30:

יראת העונש...עיקר התשובה מתחלת ממנה...לכן ממנה הוא מתחרט
ומתחיל...כי צד ההתחלה כבר אמרנו שאינה יכולה להיות כי אם
מיראת גשמיות כמותו שהיא יראת המיתה והעונש מינים ממינים
שונים שאין להאריך—אבל בה הוא מסיים ג'כ רק בדרך אחר והיא
יראת הרע המהוה המיתה והעונשים.

See also L.A., p. 36b: אנכי תמיד הוי' מדת הרחמים רוצה
While regret (חרטה) is להיטיב רק האלוקים הדינין הם מבחינתך
an indispensable point of departure for "return," it may
not be allowed to evolve into indulgence of guilt (הדינין
הם מבחינתך).

[30]L.A., p. 24b.

אודך ד' כי אנפת בי וגו' ותנחמני (ישעי' יב—יא'), דרך משל שאוהב
אדם בנו הקטן ומכה אותו מחמת אהבה, והתינוק מתחיל לבכות
וכשמתחיל לבכות אביו בצער **ומנשק אותו**, וזהו כי אנפת בי, **האף הוא
בי**, שאני סובר שזה אף, ובאמת אתה עושה מחמת אהבה. שוב אפך,
כשאפך פירוש מכתך חוזרת אצלך, כביכול כנ'ל, ותנחמני אתה מנחם
אותי.

[31]For the following see L.A., pp. 4b-5a, 8b-9a, 9b-10b.
In the secondary literature, reverence is generally understood as the contrast to fear of punishment, and the term
יראת רוממות is employed to evoke that meaning. But the

phrase, as far as could be determined, does not appear before the mid-eighteenth century. Before this period, יראה and רוממות are juxtaposed, but not as a coined phrase, and only in the following sense, for which Bahya Ibn Paquda's *Havot ha-Levavot*, gate 10, ch. 6, may serve as an example:

ותיראה על שני פנים: אחד מהם, יראת ענשו ונסיונו והשני, יראה לכבודו ורוממותו ועוצם גבורתו [של ד']

R. Mendel considers a Zoharic passage as a source for his notion of יראת הרוממות, see L.A., p. 4b, but there, too, the specific phrase is not employed. See also *D'rashot ha-Ran*, ed. A. Feldman (Jerusalem, 1974), pp. 166-167.

[32] מי שהוא בבחינת יראה נחותה שנקרא מיתה צריך לבוא אל החיות שהוא עיקר יראת ד' לחיים...

[33]*Netivot Olam* II, *Netiv Yir'at ha-Shem*, ch. 1, p. 22.

אין היראה רק שעושה עצמו עלול והוא אצלו כאלו אינו, כך היראה ד' עושה עצמו כאין אצל עלתו.

[34]*D'rush l'Shabbat ha-Gadol*, pp. 53-54.

[35]ליפות

[36]יראות חצוניות. For identification of יראה with these impulses, see L.A. pp. 20a, 27a, 14b; *Peri Etz*, pp. 25, 30, 31; *Peri ha-Aretz, Ki Tissa.*

[37]L.A., p. 3b.

[38]L.A., p. 33b:

אנכי – **אהבה** שהוציא ממצרים מכל צרות; לא יהי' – **יראה**, פי שלא תלך אחר **תאוה** שהיא אל אחר; על פני – **פי**' על פנימיות...

see n.37.

L.A., p. 40b:

וכל דבר שאדם חושק שלא לשם שמים נקרא תאוה

[39]Ibid.,

מי שיש לו מרה שחורה אינו יכול לקבל שום תענוג מחמת **גדלותו** כי **מרה הוא לשון גדלות**, וזהו גדלות של הבל, ולכן נקראת מרה שחורה – וייש גדלות הבורא ית' שהוא טוב, וזה העניין (שמות טו:כג) ויבואו מרתה ולא יכלו לשתות מים ממרה, דהיינו השכל.

[40]L.A., p. 12a. See the larger context of the passage:

באמת עיקר העבודה שיפשיט האדם עצמו מכל המבוקשים...**והכל**

תועלת עצמו...ויעתיק עצמו מכל **המדות והמבוקשים לעצמו [ימין ושמאל] רק בו יתברך.**

[41]יסתור הבנין שלו.

[42]L.A., p. 14b, the section beginning: ואפי' אם נכשל בעבירה ח'ו לא ירבה בעצבות...

[43]L.A., p. 33b:
על פני — פי' על פנימיות, שהפנימיות הוא הקב'ה וראוי ליבוש מפניו, וזהו אל מול פני המנורה — הפנימיות — יאירו שבעת הנרות, פי' שבע מדות הבנין, אהויר' ושאר כנודע.

[44]L.A., p. 26a.
והוא יתברך דבוק לנו, אך המניעה מצדנו...שהוא יתברך שורה במחשבה, וכשאדם חושב חס ושלום דברי שטות דוחה אותו יתברך.
The term "רברי שטות" is used in the sense of aberrations from the center of *devekut.*

[45]L.A., p. 14a.
עצבות כמעט כעבודה זרה, שמראה שאינו רוצה ח'ו בגזרת המלך והבורא ית"ש

[46]*Peri Etz*, p. 17:
כידוע מענין אמרו רז'ל הרשעים מלאים חרטות כשהיצ'הר מניחם ואינו מסיתם ומתחרטים מאד וכמדומם הם שלבם חלל בקרבם, ובטל היצ'הר מאתם...ולכן המה מתמיהים על שאינם מגיעים למדרגה יותר גדולה, ובאמת שעדיין לא נצח את היצ'הר ובעת מלחמה קרובים לשוב.

[47]L.A., p. 20a.
אם אמנם חושב באהבה רעה יאמר בלבו מה עשיתי...ובזה יוכנע ויבא עד עפר, ותבא זאת המחשבה למדת אין.

[48]L.A., p. 33b.
שצמצמתי מחשבתי מלחשוב בשוב דבר רק בזה [בבורא], וזו המדה נקראת אין שדוחה מחשבות אחרות.

[49]L.A., p. 40a.
וכלל הוא, דכל מי שנוגע יראת ד' בלבו צריך לעבוד את ד' **בתחלת** המחשבה תיכף כשיבוא להתעוררות, דהיינו שיחשוב במחשבתו שהוא כאין דמה שהוא כאין א'א להיות בו חסרון ושבירה קודם שיבוא לעולם הפירוד. זז'ש ועשו לי מקדש וגו', שיעשה האדם את עצמו מקדש, שיעבוד את ד' **בתחלת המחשבה,** דהיינו מחנה שכינה.

[50]L.A., pp. 9b-10a.
ואמר הבע'שט זלהה' אין ר"ל דבר שהוא אין שהוא הרצון הנקרא אין

לרוב העלם שאין משיגים אותו זהו מזל לישראל עכ׳...שהוא הרצון
והוא למעלה מזכות והוא חסד של אמת, ונקרא חסד ח׳ס ד׳ שחס על
מדריגת דלים לקרבם וזהו העיקר.

See the correlative statement, L.A., p. 37b:

והישר בעיניו תעשה שבאמת אין מזל לישראל, שהם למעלה מהמטבע,
והוא דרוש ארוך נתבאר במ׳א שזה נקרא ישר.

[51]L.A., p. 12a; L.A., p. 35b.

[52]L.A., pp. 8b, 10b.

[53]As R. Mendel cites him, the Baal Shem Tov uses the
word פניה to refer to both "right" and "left" diversions
from *devekut*; L.A., p. 16a-16b:

הבעשט׳ זלה׳ה אמר שאם לא יהי׳ לאדם **שום פני׳** שיה׳ה הכל **שוה
אצלו** בודאי זוכה לכל המדריגות...כלל גדול מהבעשט׳ זל׳ה׳ה
ההשתוות פי׳ שיה׳ה **שוה** אצלו אם ישבחוהו בני אדם או **יגנוהו** הוא
דבר גדול מאד. וכן יהי׳ שוה אצלו אם יחזיקוהו לחסרון ידיעה או ליודע
כל התורה, והדבר הגורם לזה הוא הדביקות באלקים.

There is apposition in these phrases:

שום פני׳...הכל שוה אצלו...אם ישבחוהו בני אדם או יגנוהו.

The השתוות relates to both the gratification ("right") that
comes from praise and the shame ("left") provoked by
abuse—and both of them are פניות. For another use of פני׳
in reference to the "left," see L.A., p. 35; for "right" פניות
see L.A., p. 29b.

[54]L.A., p. 21a:

דיש מתפלל **במרה שחורה** וסובר שמתפלל ביראת ד׳, וכן סובר
שמתפלל באהבת ד׳, והוא באמת **מרה אדומה.**

These terms reflect the phraseology of the "tempera-
ments" or "humors." On the biological and psychological expression of these tempers, see, for example, Meir
Aldabi's *Shvilei Emunah, Netiv* IV (Warsaw, 1887), pp.
66, 65:

—המרה השחורה...מתילדת משריפת החלטים והנטירה והנקימה
וההקפדה ורוב קנאה ורוע הלב וזועף הפנים הוא בא ממנה, וכן כשאדם
מתעצל ופותח פיו ומותח ידיו ורגליו בדאגה או בעצלות.
—וזו המרה [האדומה] היא אצל הדם...וההריצות והעזות והרוגז
והתחרות כלם באים ממנה

These two tempers are viewed in the passage as diversions from *devekut*—just as פניות are (L.A., p. 18b). These two tempers then are another way of expressing "left" and "right" diversions.

[55]L.A., p. 16a: כל פניה היא מצד גבהות.

[56]ישבחוהו בני אדם או יגנוהו.

[57]L.A., p. 16b.

כלל גדול מהבע'שט זלהה', ההשתוות פי' שיהי שוה אצלו אם ישבחוהו
בני אדם או יגנוהו הוא דבר גדול מאד, וכן יה'ה שוה אצלו אם יחזיקוהו
לחסרון ידיעה או ליודע כל התורה. והדבר הגורם לזה הוא הדבקות
באלקים שמחמת טרדת הדבקות אין לו פנאי. לחשוב בדברים אלו,
שטרוד מאד לחשוב לדבק בבורא יתברך. ובכל דבר שיעשה יחשוב
שעושה נחת רוח בזה להשכינה, ולא יחשוב במחשבתו **אפי' מעט**
לצורך הנאתו כי הבל וריק, ולמה יעשה להנאתו, וגם אם עושה כמה
דברים והכנות כדי שיוכל לעבוד בדביקות **ויהי' לו תענוג בעבודה** זו גם
זה עובד לצורך עצמו רק עיקר שתהי' כל עבודתו לצורך השכינה אפי'
מעט לא יהי' לצורך עצמו.

[58]See also L.A., p. 21b:

אחד שעובד הקב'ה מחמת תורה ומצוות ויש לו חשק יותר רק צריך
שלא יעיין על עבודה שלא יבא לידי פניה

also L.A., p. 28a:

דיש שני מיני עבירות האחד שאירע לאדם שעבר דבר, ואחד שיש לו
גאוה במה שעובד הק'בה, ונ'מ דעבירה ראשונה כשיבוא להתעוררות
תשובה—מתכפרת אבל כשיש לו גאוה, במה שבא להתעוררות
תשובה מתגאה יותר, וזה מונע מכל עבודת ד'.

[59]L.A., p. 19b

אלקיכם כהן הוא (סנהדרין לט.) פי' דאין עובדין את הש'ית אלא בכח
שנותן במחשבה ובדיבור, וזאת הוא עולם המחשבה ועולם הדיבור,
נמצא מחמת ד' עובדין אותו, וזהו הק'בה כהן, שעובד **בעצמו כ'י את**
עצמו.

[60]L.A., p. 26b-27a

לעולם יאחז אדם עצמו כי הוא רק כמגריפה שהיא עור ויש בה נקבים
ודרך שם יוצא קול הזמר, וכי תתגאה העור מה שיוצא ממנה קול זמר?
כך האדם המחי' ברוך הוא, וכל המדות הכל שורים בו כבתוך כלי, ומה
יתגאה, הוא בעצמו אינו כלום, ואין בו רק מדות רעות, והוא מחויב
להעלות אותן להש'ית.

[61]*Peri Etz*, p. 14:

כשמקבל היסורים באהבה אמתית, בהשגתו הלא ד' הוא הטוב הגנוז
כנ"ל א"א להשיג טובתו אז טוב לו להיות מתקשר בחכמה **שהרי כשאינו**
מצטער מן היסורים יצא מכלל הגוף ונתקשר בחכמה. וזהו שאמרו רז"ל
סמא דיסורים שתיקותא, **כי השתיקה היא התקשרות** החכמה כאמר סיג
לחכמה שתיקה וזהו ענין גם זו לטובה, וזהו ענין קיבול היסורים
באהבה.

[62]See n.57.

[63]P. 16b.

[64]*Peri Etz*, pp. 22-26.

[65]P. 24; see also L.A., pp. 19b and 27b:

מי שהוא עניו אזי הוא למעלה מן המדות וזהו (דניאל ב:כב) ידע מה
בחשוכא הקב"ה', מתקשר עצמו עם מי שמחזיק עצמו **למה** בחשוכא,
אפי' בין הרשעים, ונהורא עמי שרא, נהורא, אור זרוע לצדיק, האור
שלמעלה מן המדות עמו שורה, כי מחזיק עצמו לאין ואינו במדה,
לפיכך הוא ית' שוכן את דכא ושפל רוח, וגם זה הוא מדת ענותנותו ית'
דהא הוא גדול גבור ונורא, והאדם שפל וחוטא, אעפ' שורה עם האדם.
[66]

וכל מה שהוא מתלהב ביותר ומשיג בלבו אמיתות הענין אשר לא
מנפשו היא כי מה עשה ובמה יוכל לעשות ככה, מגודל עכירות גשמיות
נפשו ומחשבתו, אבל רוח ד' דיבר בו...ואהבתו (ז.א. חיותו, כדלהלן)
הלא זה אוד מוצל מאש.

Ibid., p. 24, for another passage where התלהבות is used
in this sense, see L.A., pp. 19b-20a:

ואם מתפלל בהתלהבות אז יראה על המ"ז מה היא...אם באהבה רעה
כגון ניאוף יביא יביא אותה אל שרשה שהיא אהבת ד'...יאמר בלבו מה
עשיתי שלקחתי חלק מעולמות המחשבה ל מקום הטנופת, ובזה יכנע
ויבא עד עפר, ותבא זאת המחשבה למדת אין

התלהבות is not employed in relation to religious service
prior to Hasidism, and its philology requires further
study. The discussion in the article is an attempt to suggest approaches to the term's genesis. It may be inferred
from Ben Yehuda's and Kenaani's dictionaries that the
reflexive form of להב is rare. When it is used prior to the
mid-eighteenth century, it is to denote "burning" pain:

וכאשר תהיה תהיה המורסא ההיא תחת היד חמה והיה מראהו אדום ויהיה

לחולה קדחת רצמא וניחור בלשון עם כאב חזק והנה זה אות כי **המורסא
חמה מתלהבת**:

(Shvilei Emunah, p. 88) This is actually the first sense of
התלהבות, employed by R. Mendel; Hasidic usage converts
the physiological sense to an emotional one.
[67]

אז יתלהב...יותר ויותר...ולא יספוק ימים דיו לבאר עוצם וגודל חללה
של לב האוהב אמיתי...בלהב השמחה.

Ibid. For this second sense of התלהבות, see also ibid., p.
25:

שהרי חיות הנמשך ומקושר בדבר היא האהבה וממילא מתלהב עליו
אהבתו יתברך, וחוט של חסד משוך עליו.

[68]The text goes on:

והראיה באם העדר האהבה זו, הרי הוא ככל אדם בעניני הגשמ־
ים...והנה בהיותו במדה זו הרי היא כאותו אדם, ובמדה זו הרי כאותו
בעל תאוה, וממילא אוהב כל ישראל אפי' לרשעי ישראל, מפני
אמיתות הבנתו וידיעתו שקרובים המה לו, ויש לו שייכות עמהם, והנה
הוא כאחד האדם ואין לו לעצמו ויתרון עליהם כי אם מה שענוהו
כשערה מן השמים.

[69]Ibid., p. 25

וזהו שויתי ד' לנגדי תמיד. פי' שהוא משוה את ד' אפי' בכל התנגדות
המזמן אליו **או ראה או ידע** מאמין במאמר ואתה מחי' את כולם.
Leviticus 5:1 (או ראה או ידע) is an allusion to *Zohar* passage
developed by the Magid of Mezeritch as well.

See *Magid D'varav l'Yaakov*, ed. R. Schatz (Jerusalem,
1976), p. 64 (section 42):

וזהו (ויקרא ה:א) נפש כי חחטא. אורייתא קא מתמה. היאך אפשר
שתחטא, ושמעה קול אלה, ה'ה לו לשמוע קול של השבועה. **או ראה**,
שרואה מעשים של א' ונזכר במעשיו, דכל מה שאדם רואה ישים אל
לבו למה הראה לי הק'בה את זה, הלא הכל בהשגחה פרטית. אלא אם
רואה דבר עבירה יחשוב מסתמא גם אני עשיתי שמץ מנהו, אעפ' שלא
עשה כזה ממש. למשל אם הוא רואה את אחד שבא על אשת איש
והוליד ממזר, ומוציא זדע לבטלה ע'י מחשבה זרה, חמור כמו מוליד
ממזר. וזהו **או ראה**, שרואה דבר עבירה מאדם אחר ונזכר דבר שעשה.
או ידע, ע'ד בושנו במעשינו ונכלמנו להרים פנינו אליך...

The passage in *Zohar* to which the *Magid* relates is part
III, 13b:

או ראה, אינון חובין דעבד ואסתכל בהו; או ידע בבירורא דמלה דעבר
על פקודא דמארי' אם לא יגיד, אם לא יודי עליהו קמי מארי' כד יפוק
מהאי עלמא, ונשא עונו.

[70]An entire sermon in *Peri Etz (Va-Yetze*, pp. 7-9) is
devoted to this theme. See, for example, pp. 7-8:

ומעתה בכל מאורעות העולם חייב אדם לומר בשבילי, שכן האמת,
וביד כל אדם לתקן המאורע עי' יחוד קב'הוש בעצמו...והנה מעין
המאורע בעולם ידע איניש בנפשו איך הוא נגד ד' — שהרי **העולם הנה**
הוא בעצמו בשבילו נברא ומתקיים ומתנהג לפי דרכו ובכל מקום...מ-
משלת אדונו שם, ובאמרו כי בורח הוא מייסרים אותו שם...והנה האדם
שאמר שבשבילו נברא העולם וכן היא מתנהג לפי דרך הנהגתו לפני ד'
ומעין המארע בעולם מבין החסרון שבעצמו ורואה לשוב עד ד'

[71]P. 25 (2nd col.) on 'פחד ד; p. 24 (2nd col) and p. 25a
(2nd col.) on voice of God; see also L.A., p. 32b:

ושמעתי בשם רי'בש...וכן אם שומע או מדבר ומתפלל יאמר מה הביאו
הלום ד' לדבר בתוך תפלה, הלא כל זה בהשגחה פרטית, אך הדיבור
הוא השכינה, ושרתה כביכול השכינה בפה של זה האדם כדי שיזדרז
עצמו לעבודה. כמה יש לחזק עצמו בעבודה זו, ובפרט אם זה האיש
שמדבר נכרי או קטן. נמצא צמצמה עצמה השכינה כביכול בזה האדם,
כמה ראוי לעשות בזריזות, עכ'ד

L.A. 18b

כשדנין את ישראל כביכול דנין אותו יתברך, שהוא אחדות עמנו.
[72]*Peri Etz*, p. 26.
[73]See *Bava Mezia* 47a.
[74]*Peri Etz*, p. 25

וכל הנקרא בשמו ולכבודו אפי' כל ההתנגדות וזה ד' — אדם שחטא,
ד' — אחר שיחטא, א-ל-המעלה את הכל, ומתחילה ועד סוף הכל הוא
ית' בעצמו, ומה לאדם שיבא אחר המלך למה זה הוא כך וזה הוא כך,
ואין לו לאדם כי אם **לסדר שבחו יתברך לפניו כמו סודר [חליפין]**
בעלמא, וממילא תעשה הכל...אפי' תחלת יראתו מפניך מאתך אני.
[75]*Nezah Yisrael*, ch. 15, p. 89; *Derush l'Shabbat ha-*
Gadol, p. 90.
[76]*Peri Etz*, p. 26.

שאם היה מקשר עצמו במדות היראה אליו ית' הוה אתי מטרא, פי'
המשכה ושפע חיות שמחי' היראה היא מדת האהבה שהיא שפע
[77]Ibid., p. 25; see also L.A., p. 32b:

וכן ביראה אם ירא מע׳כום או מחרב יאמר בלבו מה יש לי לירא מאדם
כמוני, בודאי הק׳בה מלובש בזה האדם, וכמה יש לי לירא ממנו עצמו

[78]This is called מסירת נפש.

[79]Ibid., p. 25, col. 2.

[80]שופטים...תתן לך...פי׳ בעצמך.

[81]Ibid., p. 26, col. 2.

[82]*Ibid.* פשט הגשם is of course identical to R. Mendel's
references to התפשטות הגשמיות, which leads, he emphasizes, to an unequivocal sense of the divine. See the remarkable passage in L.A., p. 21a:

אמנם אה׳ויר [דביקות] א׳א לבוא אליו **רק כשמאמין שהשית׳ לפניו
מדבר בדחילו ורחימו כמו שמבין** אז תפול עליו יראה עד שיופשט
מגשמיות, וכשתהא לו האמונה שזאת השכינה היא היראה היא
השכינה ילך להלאה ויבא לפנים הנראים וכשילך להלאה יבא לפנים
שאינם נראים,

וזהו (ד׳ה א׳ כח:ט) דע את אלקי אביך גו׳, **שתהא מקושר אליו
בהתפשטות הגשמיות, ותהא רואה שיש אלקים בעולם**, ואף אם הכופ־
רים אומרים מנא לך הא, לא יציית אותם, כמשל א׳ ראה בגשמיות
שדבר זה הוא זהב אעפ׳ שאומרים לו שאינו זהב, אעפכ׳ הוא יודע
האמת שהוא זהב, כך כשרואה בעין שכלו את השית׳ לא מפסיד
באמונתו שום דבר.

[83]Ibid. This theme (psychologization of the *sephirot*) is
frequently discussed; namely, the relation between the
seven primary feelings, their elevation as שבעת ימי הבנין,
and their root in the supernal realm. See, for example,
L.A., p. 19b:

דיש שבעה מחשבות ולא יותר, וזהו ז׳ ימי הבנין ובכ׳א יש ערב ובוקר,
ערב–לשון תערובות שחושב מחשבות חיצוניות, ובוקר–לשון
בקרות, שמבקר את השית׳ ואלה הם, אהבת ד׳ ואהבת העברות, ויראת
ד׳ ויראה רעה, כגון שנאה, והתפארות שמפאר ד׳. ורעה הוא שמפאר
א׳ע, ונצוח והודי׳ ויסוד ל׳ התקשרות.

and L.A., pp. 43b, 20b. On psychologization of *sephirot*
in early Hasidism, see. G. Scholem, *Major Trends in
Jewish Mysticism*, last chapter.

[84]L.A., pp. 35b-36a:

כ׳ז שמתגדל ומתרחב שפעו, הרי כל העולמות מלאים טוב והוא מתגדל

בעולמו, וע'ז אנחנו מתפללים שיתרחב גבול הקדושה וימלא כבודו כל הארץ ואז ממילא הטוב יהיה בעצמו

והעיקר הוא שיתגדל שמו עיז', וכל כוונתנו רק להשי'ת בכל שאלותינו

[85]See, for example, L.A., p. 31a:

משה רבנו ע'ה...והי' תמיד דבוק להמחשבה ולא היה הפסיק בין משה שלמעלה למשה שלמטה, **וכל דבר שראה— ראה את השי'ת**, ולא היתה לו בשוב פעם מחשבה זרה.

אלו ואלו דברי אלקים חיים[86]

מחלקת לשם שמים סופה להתקיים[87]

[88]For the cognate discussion of *Avot* 5:18-19 by both Maharal and R. Mendel, see *Derek Hayim*, pp. 605-610; *Peri ha-Aretz*, pp. 48-52; L.A., p. 36b; *Peri Etz* on *Ki Teizei*.

[89]Related to the failed effort which connects one to the Source, R. Mendel stresses that *devekut* cannot be attained artificially. That is, it will not do to induce a feeling of humility in a vacuum. The challenge to self-satisfaction must come as the result of a happening which "befalls" one: a lapse or provocation which produces "fears" (in the generic sense) and—through acquiescence —is related as "fear of heaven" and becomes a "chariot" for the divine (L.A., p. 27a).

עובד ד'...בדחילו (יראה) ורחימו (אהבה), ויראה היא שתפולנה עליו יראה ורעדה מחמת פחד, ולא מחמת שמעורר עליו יראה, כי זהו רק העלאת מ'נ

L.A., p. 22a. The larger context of these lines is the identification of two modes of divine service:

הא' מחמת תורה ותפלה מתחזק יותר לעבודת השי'ת...ויקרא אפרים שפרו ורבו מחמת מצוות

The second is the rubric under which the cited passage is considered:

ויש עוד מדרגה הנקרא מנשה לשון שכחה...ששוכח בהקבה'...והאדם יתן אל לבו הלא לא עבדתי את ד'

This "forgetfulness" is concomitant with a lapse, an "alien" thought:

כשנפלה לאדם ז'ז אז יתבושש עד מאד כי דחפו אותו מהיכל מלך,

וישוב לתוך ההיכל **בבושה רבה** ובהכנעה גדולה כי מ׳ז היא עבירה
גדולה

(L.A., p. 20a):

אם אמנם חושב באהבה רעה **יאמר בלבו מה עשיתי** שלקחתי חלק
מעולמות המחשבה אל מקום הטנופת, ובזה יוכנע ויבא עד עפר, ותבא
זאת המחשבה למדת אין ואח׳כ תבוא לעולם האהבה, בזכרו אם אני
אוהב הדבר הזה...כמה יש לי לאהוב את השי׳ת

(L.A., p. 20a) The "בושה" and the realization of "מה
התלהבות. אהבה רעה צריך להעלות, p. 18a, עשיתי"
ביראה (in the first sense) is meaningful in such situations
because one has experienced one's אין through יראה (as
just defined)

ופעמים אין יכול האדם לעבוד השי׳ת מחמת שאין לו שכל...מה
תקנתו?...בהתלהבות, שנופלת על האדם התלהבות גדולה שאפי׳ אדם
פשוט יכול לבוא למדרגה זו כי המדרגה הזאת אינה מחמת עובדא, לכן
יכולים לבוא לה, וצריך להעמיד עצמו לאין, שכשהוא חושב עצמו ליש
אז אין הקבה׳ מתלבש בו...אבל כשהוא חושב שהוא אין ושוכח
בעצמו...ואין דבוק כלל בתאות עו׳הז, אז הוא יכול לבוא למעלה
מהזמן...ששם הכל שוים...אבל אדם הדבוק בטבעיות עו׳הז, אינו יכול
להתפשט מגשמיות כשהוא מתאוה לאיזה דבר.

The context indicates that when R. Mendel says

כשהוא חושב שהוא אין ושוכח בעצמו...ואין דבוק כלל בתאות עו׳הז
the תאוה is not coming from the "right" but from the
"left"—(as תאוה is used in L.A., p. 33b: פי׳. יראה. — לא יהיה
שלא תלך אחר תאוה שהיא אל אחר). In other words, the lapse
gives rise to התלהבות (in the first sense) rather than to a
sinister "desire" for grief or resentment. The sense of אין
in this passage, then, complements the meanings sampled
in the body of the text (in particular, אין as exclusive
preoccupation with the divine). It means, here, *oblivion* to
impulses right and left (hence, **שוכח בעצמו**). In this way,
there is no attachment to טבעיות עו׳הז, enabling one to be
"beyond time" (מעל הזמן).

To go back to the initial passage cited in this note,
עבודה בדחילו ורחימו, or באה׳ויר—*the most frequently used
term in R. Mendel's writing*—*refer to these themes.* יראה,
for R. Mendel, as for Maharal refers to the state of אין.

When one is אין, the "positive" content of religious feelings will be genuine (לשמה), without "right" or "left"
digressions (פניות):

L.A., p. 36a—לשמה בלי שום פני'

L.A., p. 18b—דבור באה'ויר' ולא בפני'

L.A., p. 40b—in light of the just cited comment on תאוה,
see p. 40b, תאוה...וכל דבר שאדם חושק שלא לש'ש לבד היא. In
אין, one is both reconciled (avoiding perils of the left) and
chastened (avoiding those of the right). Transferring to
the realm beyond time, one experiences its bliss, i.e., the
divine life, sustaining one in אין:

וכשיגיע ליראת ד' יבין וישכיל אם אמנם היראה היא פחד ד' הלא גם זה
המדה נבראת מאתו ית'ש ויש בה חיות מאתו ית' שא'א בלתו ואם
נמשך לה חיות ממקום גבוה ממילא מצומצם בתוכה אהבה. שהרי
חיות הנמשך ומקושר בדבר היא האהבה, וממילא מתלהב עליו אהבתו
ית'

The last phrase (וממילא מתלהב עליו אהבתו), correlated with
the earlier use of התלהבות in this note, indicates that
worship, בדחילו ורחימו, is synonymous with the dual
awareness of התלהבות, discussed in the body of the text. It
is this notion that is developed in early Hasidic thought as
העלאת מ'ז. On this notion, see the chapter on elevating
alien thoughts in L. Jacobs, *Hasidic Prayer* (New York,
1972).

ייראה is the gate to אהבה; and if one does not pass
through it, how can love possibly come about? L.A., p.
22a:

יראה היא שער לאהבה אם אינו נכנס בשער שהוא יראה איך אפשר
להיות באהבה

דחילו ורחימו is an inseparable unit: without יראה one's
אהבה is mere self-worship (L.A., p. 16b): ...יהיה לו תענוג
יראה. בעבודה זו, גם זה עובד לצורך עצמו. Without divine love,
degenerates into misery and self-pity L.A. (p. 21a), יש
מתפלל במרה שחורה. וסובר שמתפלל ביראת ד'.

Another perspective on this discussion is the theme of דבר והפוכו (formulated thus in *Peri Etz*, p. 19). So pervasive in Maharal, it is frequently employed by R. Mendel as well. One perceives the light (אהבה) only after having passed through the "darkness" of the fall (יתרון האור מן החישך). See pp. 41b-42a for several illustrations. This sensation of divine support inferred from a recognition of one's lapses and failing is poignantly expressed in this passage (*Peri Etz*, p. 7):

צריך שיהי' לבו רואה את הערוה ארציות שלו, איש אדמה, ואיך הוא רחוק מד' בכל דרכיו מגושם ומגשם חיות הקדש...והכתוב אומר כולם בחכמה עשית, ואם חכמה אין כאן, במה יתקיים? וזהו סיבת מאורעות העולם ליסר את האדם לשוב עד ד' בכל לבו ומלאה הארץ דעה את ד', כל חד וחד לפום שיעורא דיליי

Compare this notion with Maharal's comment on *Avot* 1:10 concerning מסתפק בעצמו. Successful attainment of this goal (described as נהנה מיגיע כפו explained as נהנין מזיו השכינה) results in a love for God who sustained the effort. effort.

אי אפשר גם כן שלא יאהב מי שחנן לו דבר זה, כי מי שנותן מתנה לאחר, ואותה מתנה מקובלת ואהובה על המקבל ביותר, איך אפשר שלא יאהב מאד מי שנותן המתנה אליו.

    🌿   🌿

R. Mendel stresses the meaningfulness of worship בד'ור (L.A., p. 22a):

ישוב אל ד' בכל כוחו ולבבו זהו נקרא מנשה, כי מחמת ששכח את ד' עובד יותר.

But he rejects initiating "falls" (Sabbatian and Frankist style); he simply urges responding to those that befall one: L.A., pp. 12b-13a:

וכן בכל הדברים צריך האדם שיהא עובד ד' תמיד עבודת גבוה, ולא כמו המתפקרים ח'ו שאומרים שצריך האדם להיות יורד במדרגה התחתונה ומשם יעלה למעלה, ירידה צורך עלי', לא תהא כזאת בישראל. וכמה יצאו מהדת עבור זה, ולכן יהיה האדם תמיד דבוק בו יתברך שמו. ואם ח'ו נופל ממדרגה צריך במהרה לשוב למעלה, והדברים ארוכים לבארם כי אין זה בכח האדם, שאם יעשה כן יפול ולא יקום.

The ideology opposed by R. Mendel here is that recon-
structed by G. Scholem, "Mitzvah ha-Baah ba'Aveirah,"
Knesset II (1937).

Complementing the above citation from L.A., see also
Peri Etz, p. 32:

והלכה כר׳א דאין אדם רשאי להכניס עצמו לידי נסיון, אבל כשבא לידו
נסיון פתאום ופתע בלא דעת, ישתמש במדת הגבורות והסתלקות
למעלה אל שרשו, וזה קיום הבריאה.

(Stressed here once again is that connection to the Source
occurs through "arrest" of "fears" or "loves").

[90]*Peri ha-Aretz*, pp. 34-35.

[91]שלם עם ד׳.

[92]Maharal's *Gevurot ha-Shem*, pp. 296-297, for relation
between הודאה and ד׳ השלמה אל ד׳.

[93]סבות.

[94]*P'ri ha-Aretz*, p. 35:

ולא יסמוך במה שלא עבר עבירה מימיו, הרי מסתמא כל כחותיו
קשורים בו ית׳ שאין ראיה לדבר, כי אולי לא בא לידי נסיון, או מחמת
שארי דברים המונעים אותו **כמו הבושה או מה שיהיה מעתה** מה בכך
שלא עבר עבירה הכתובה, אם שורש העון עצמו אינו נמחק מלבו, הרי
קשור הוא בו

[95]תשובה.

[96]Ibid.

[97]L.A., p. 44b.

[98]מעל הזמן.

[99]

והרבה דברי מוסר אשר הם בתלמוד אשר מיסרים האדם בדרכים
הטובים והישרים ראיתי לחבר אותם ביחד, ואין כונתנו רק לחבר
המאמרים　　ולפרש דברי חכמים לא זולת כלל עד שהחבור הזה אינו רק
פירוש דברי חכמים שבאו בתלמוד כמו שפרשנו מסכת אבות.

[100]L.A., p. 13a.

CENTER FOR JEWISH STUDIES

HARVARD JUDAIC MONOGRAPHS

HARVARD JUDAIC TEXTS AND STUDIES